The Foundation of Profitable Dentistry

The
Foundation
of Profitable
Dentistry

A Complete Guide to
Building & Sustaining Profitability
Through Any Crisis

Bita Saleh, D.D.S.

NEW YORK

LONDON • NASHVILLE • MELBOURNE • VANCOUVER

The Foundation of Profitable Dentistry

A Complete Guide to Building & Sustaining Profitability Through Any Crisis

Published in New York, New York, by Morgan James Publishing. Morgan James is a trademark of Morgan James, LLC. www.MorganJamesPublishing.com

ISBN 9781631951725 paperback
ISBN 9781631951732 eBook
Library of Congress Control Number: 2020937677

Cover Design by:
Christopher Kirk
www.GFSstudio.com

Interior Design by:
Chris Treccani
www.3dogcreative.net

Morgan James is a proud partner of Habitat for Humanity Peninsula and Greater Williamsburg. Partners in building since 2006.

Get involved today! Visit
MorganJamesPublishing.com/giving-back

TABLE OF CONTENTS

CHAPTER 1:

It Wasn't Supposed to Be This Way

I t is not by accident that you're here, reading these words. It's probably because something about this book aligned with part of your energy, either with what you have experienced in the past or what you hope to experience in the future. Either way, you are in the right place. This book is written about you and for you so that you no longer feel alienated from the profession you've chosen to dedicate your life to.

History teaches us what is possible under certain conditions. It is for this reason that I start this book with a review of a common path that you, as a dentist, may have traveled, from being a dental student to becoming a practice owner and beyond. There are a certain few and fleeting moments in a dentist's life when opportunities for pause and reflection present. When you choose to stop running and doing and instead take the time to be present in these moments, you gain the clarity to make those tough decisions that have the inherent power to positively change the trajectory of your practice and its profitability. In this chapter, we will take a look at these moments and their significance. The details of the path are not as important as the reflections. If you are a dentist reading this, you may resonate with parts of this path and not others. Everyone's story is different, so I encourage you to take what resonates with you and let the rest go in order to be open and present and fully consider the reflections.

Like most dentists, you may have worked your entire life with one goal in mind: to be a dentist and your own boss. The artistic part of dentistry allows your right brain to exercise creativity, and the science part allows your left brain to deliver excellent dentistry. You have always known that there are other professions in which you can make more money, but to make a difference and help people, you have chosen dentistry.

You most likely have a type A personality. This type of personality is required, welcomed, and fostered to get through dental school's curriculum. In fact, your training reinforces this type A personality for survival. However, to excel, you not only have to work hard, but you also have to learn to swallow your pride in the face of negative comments and stay up at night redoing project after project to fulfill the practical portion of the day, before going on to complete the academic portion.

At some point along this path, you suddenly realize that you have long ago said goodbye to the person you used to be—the person who had time to sleep in on weekends and take showers in the morning, the person who had time to dress with a sense of style before leaving to get to class. There are no mealtimes anymore because you eat when you can, and as long as what you eat makes you full, you don't have time to pay attention to what you're putting in your body. Not paying attention to what you eat was interrupted in the first year when you were required to dissect a human body in the anatomy lab. Although you felt immense gratitude for the generosity of the humans who donated their physical body for the sake of your education, you could not get used to the foul smell from the material that preserved the bodies. The smell would follow you for days afterward as if it had penetrated your skin and washing it with soap multiple times had no effect. The endless removal of fat to find the nerves and the muscles might have affected your ability to eat chicken or meat for a while, or it may have led you to become a vegetarian by default.

Although the hurdles you encountered every day tested you again and again, there was also a deep feeling of satisfaction from being able to successfully jump from one adversity to another. Your goal of becoming a dentist always remained front and center in your mind as the driving force that propelled you forward. You agreed with yourself to be selfless and to sacrifice and to do whatever was needed to get through the program.

Another aspect of your personality is that you are persistently dedicated to setting and keeping your goals. You live your life according to a plan that primarily values selflessness and self-sacrifice as paths to success. The next professional goal after graduation is to continue your education in a general practice residency or a specialty program or enter the business world by working for another dentist, purchasing an established practice, or starting a new practice. At this point in your path, it's nearly impossible to have the knowledge to know what to look for to be successfully employed or to purchase a practice that is right for you. Unless you have the money to hire a coach or consultant or have a family member who is also a dentist with experience and the willingness to share those experiences, it is certain that you will make countless mistakes. Within that first year is when you will discover the mistakes you made but you also realize you had no choice but to blindly dive in to make enough money to pay your loans and support yourself. You fall back on the agreement you made with yourself, the one of selflessness and self-sacrifice. You remind yourself that with continued hard work, one day soon you will have your profitable dream practice.

If you've been working for someone else, you decide with what you've seen out there so far that you either need to work for yourself or walk away from your dream of being a practicing dentist who owns their own business. By now, you're sick of working for others who offer you very little compensation for your hard work and, because of this, you finally find the courage and the means to purchase or start your own practice.

You are now a business owner who has to run a business that you have no training to run. The pride of ownership, the glory, and the elation of this stage last for maybe a couple of hours after you take possession of the keys to your new practice. You tell yourself that you'll do what everybody else before you has done; if all those people could do it, so can you. You tell yourself that the solution is simple: You just need to schedule patients, treat patients, collect money, pay your bills, and do it in a way that is profitable. You soon find that this simple formula has many factors affecting its success. It goes beyond self-sacrifice, selflessness, and working hard. You now have to understand what payroll is and how to effectively work with employees who you have no idea how to manage and patients who most likely will not accept all your treatment recommendations. Meanwhile, the bills pile up. The agreement that you made with yourself years ago, the one that got you through many hurdles and hard times in dental school, the one that served you so well for all these years, is no longer enough. The hardest thing to do now is to accept that the promise you made to yourself, the agreement you had with yourself to work hard and be selfless and self-sacrifice, is no longer serving you. But you realize it's too hard to completely walk away from this agreement and come up with an entirely new one. In a perfect world, coming up with a new agreement would be the best way, but as human beings going through life, it's easier to take small steps. Change is hard, so, you modify the agreement. Instead of admitting to yourself, "1) I have no idea how to run a successful and profitable business because it's beyond my training; 2) In the same way that I went to dental school to learn to become a dentist, I now need to get help to learn how to run a business successfully and profitably; 3) I will gladly accept the cost of this training because I see huge and unbelievable value in it," you say, "I will do it myself by working even harder than I did before."

The problem is that as a high-achieving, smart, determined, hard-working dentist, it is so difficult to lay your sword down and say what you know deep down to be true, "Even though I have reached this point that I always wanted to reach, I now realize that I can't do it all by myself. I need help." Asking for help is the single most difficult decision that dentists have to make. By this point, your identity is so wrapped up in what others think of you—how you know everything and can figure everything out on your own. After all, you're a doctor, and no one told you that graduating from dental school does not mean that your training is complete. No one told you that your training to become a great practicing dentist may be over (as long as you keep up with the continuing education requirements), but how to be a successful dentist who runs a successful business is just starting.

By now, you might be in your early to mid-thirties. Most of your non-dentist friends have established jobs with families and nice cars. You realize you're starting over again by embracing your own practice, and that is a hard pill to swallow. However, you decide that you have no extra money to hire a coach/consultant and it's too late to go back to school because you've invested everything you had to get to this point in your life. Even if you could hire a coach/consultant, you don't know how to evaluate whether the person is qualified or right for you. There are simply too many unknowns, so you decide to do it yourself, as you have always done. You put your social life on hold, put finding the right partner on hold (unless you already have a partner), reduce or postpone family time, and your entire life becomes your work. You carry on like this for another ten to fifteen years. You have many successes, but they pale against the mistakes you make.

One day, you realize that you can no longer continue being so tired. You are so drained that you don't recognize yourself anymore. You wonder when the last time you were happy was, and you have no answer for that. You're in your mid to late forties now, and your body is changing. You can no longer work the insane hours that you used to. You're noticing aches and pains that you never had before. You look at the production and collection numbers in your practice and ask yourself why you're not more profitable. You've worked so hard and you've given this practice everything you have. Why is it that you still have to work an insane number of hours? You don't even know who you are if you don't work constantly. You feel guilty taking time off now because your life has always been endless work, forsaking everything you might need as a person with a body and feelings and emotions. Your production is good, but what no one knows is that the overhead is high too. Money comes in and goes right back out, so you have to keep working insanely long hours to keep up, and you don't see the end or solution to this misery. The same question and dream in different forms keeps repeating itself: "What happened to my dream? Why hasn't it happened yet?" or "Who hijacked my dream?" or "If only I was more profitable, I could finally have the life I always wanted." You are now worried about not being young anymore and the new thought, in addition to the thought of not being as profitable as you once dreamed, is, "I'm losing time!"

You can't talk to anyone about these thoughts because they make you look weak. If people knew that you're not as profitable as you project or they expect, they will ask why, as though there is something wrong with you. The last thing you want is to feel judged by your friends, family, and society. Instead of asking for help, you feel more and more alone.

Managing a dental practice is difficult work. Performing dentistry on human beings who are aware of everything that is going on inside their mouths and around them is difficult. What dentists do, unlike surgeons, is surgery after surgery without having the luxury of their patients being sedated by an anesthesiologist so that they can do their job without worrying about their patient's comfort or having to manage their traumas, which are triggered every time they enter a dentist's office. It's incredibly challenging to deal with those aspects of the job and learn how to make your business more profitable.

If you have never heard that asking for help is required in your profession, let me be the first to tell you with all the love in my heart that it is not only required but is a necessity. Asking for help for yourself and your practice is the most courageous thing you can do. You are a human too! Being a doctor doesn't mean that you are a superhuman whose knowledge extends to all areas of expertise outside of your primary profession. It also doesn't mean that you're immune to the stress of consistently low profits. It means that being both a great dentist and a profitable practice owner requires some guidance from professionals and experts who can help you run a consistently profitable business. After diagnosing a patient's dentition, the next step is to get the patient to accept your treatment recommendations and show up for appointments to complete their treatment. Your expertise will not be of any use if your patients don't accept all or most of your recommendations. You may be the best dentist in the area, but if your patients are not accepting your treatment recommendations, how much of a difference do you think you can make in their health? How profitable can your practice be with a low treatment acceptance rate?

Being selfless and sacrificing yourself, as you did to be accepted into dental school and get through the program, is no longer on the table if you want to realize your dream of running a profitable dental practice. I invite you to pause and reflect on these questions:

- How can I show up as my whole self and provide better value for my patients while increasing profit and decreasing hours?
- Which one of the sacrifices that I've made for my business no longer serve me?
- How do I benefit from being on an island and not seeking help from a certified coach or consultant to attain more—and consistent—profitability?
- What will I have to give up for a more profitable practice?

- What will I gain from a more profitable practice?
- What does a consistently profitable practice say about me?
- How will a more profitable practice change my life?
- Am I ready for change and more profitability?
- What if nothing changes?
- Who am I outside of what I do?"

You have reached the fork in the road where you either reflect on these questions now or reflect on them when love and joy has been sucked out of your life and you feel stuck in a practice that brings you countless problems and misery in exchange for very little profit. Let me give you a hint: The second path does not ever involve having a profitable practice. Please choose the first one.

Reflection Points:

1. The reflection questions above are a great place to start your reflections in addition to the ones below.
2. Describe three agreements you made with yourself while in dental school?
3. Have these agreements changed over time? If Yes, why did they need to be changed?
4. Describe three agreements that you currently hold with yourself? Why is each one important? What purpose does each one serve?
5. If you were to change one agreement that you currently hold, which one would it be? How will changing this help you?

CHAPTER 2:

My Story

For years, I was just like any other dental student with a type A personality: extremely good at being selfless, hardworking, and goal-oriented, believing that the only path to success and profitability was one mired in self-sacrifice.

I followed the traditional path of finishing dental school, following it with a one-year general practice residency, and being hired right out of school as an associate dentist in a private dental practice where the owner took advantage of the fact that I had no experience in business and underpaid me. I was so glad that I had a job right after graduation that I didn't care how much I was being paid as long as I was being paid. Even if I had cared, I had no idea how much I should be getting paid.

Within ten months, I discovered that he was paying his hygienist more than me. That paired with the vast difference in our values led me to give him my two-month notice. And that vast difference was that I didn't believe patient care should be compromised for profitability.

By then, it was also clear that I should not be underpaid and undervalued. To top it off, he wanted me to agree to an insurance plan where if anything happened to him that resulted in his demise, his wife would be paid one million dollars by the insurance plan and I would own the practice. My memory is hazy on the details, but that was the essence of it. In effect, he valued his practice at one million dollars regardless of what shape it might be in at the time of his assumed demise, and I would remain an underpaid associate under his employment during that entire time. He was shocked and surprised to hear me say "no" to his perfectly self-serving plan. It was as though his idea of me as a naïve female who knew nothing about business and contracts, someone he could easily take advantage of, shattered right in front of him with that one simple "no" followed by my resignation. During the unpleasant events of that year, I had hoped that none of his decisions had anything to do with my being a single female. However, within one month of leaving his practice, I attended a study group meeting where most of the middle-aged male dentists who had heard him brag were looking to hire a single young female dentist right out of school for that exact reason: It was easier to manipulate and underpay a young single female than a young single male associate dentist. And I started to piece together a picture of the vast array of compromises in values some dentists were willing to make for profitability.

At this juncture, I was certain that I was not willing to compromise my values for profitability. I refused to believe that the only way to be profitable was to undermine patient care and take advantage of naïve dentists fresh out of school. I also knew that after what I had experienced in his practice, the only way to create a culture where profitability was not tied to compromised values was to start my own practice. It took six months to find a small dental practice that was close to home and small enough for me to comfortably handle as a first-time business owner. The process of securing a loan from a bank so that I could purchase the practice was difficult because I had no idea how to present a business plan that made sense to the banks. I thought all that was required was to visit the bank, let them know I was a licensed dentist, and ask for a loan to purchase an existing dental practice. After visiting close to twenty banks and hearing "no" repeatedly, I started to realize how difficult it was to get a loan. During that time, the economy was low. Banks were not loaning money to any doctors, let alone young doctors taking over an existing practice with no financial backing.

With the help of a generous co-signer who believed in me I was finally able to secure a bank loan. At first, I was ecstatic and grateful to be able to purchase a practice where the owner was retiring after thirty years of practicing. That meant lots of goodwill would be present. It meant his patients trusted him and therefore were likely to stay with me because he was recommending me. However, my excitement didn't last very long. In fact, it turned into sheer panic when, soon after being handed the keys, one of the patients in the practice walked in with her crown in her hand, which had been cemented only a week ago. Upon examining the patient, I realized there was not enough sound tooth structure present to support a crown and that crown should have never been made with those existing conditions. Every day I found myself having to face the fact that supervised neglect had been handed down to me by the prior dentist. I had heard about supervised neglect in dental school. But no one ever told me how to claw myself out of it when it was handed to me by my predecessor. How do I tell these patients who trusted this dentist for thirty years that the work he did was below the standard of care and the only way to fix it required a completely different treatment plan that would cost them thousands of dollars more? And how could I hope to make a profit while digging myself out of this prior dentist's hole?

Meanwhile, I stumbled upon another inaccurate piece of information given to me by the prior dentist: He had stated that he didn't accept any HMO or PPO plans in his practice. I didn't know how to check for this because the reports he handed me were all done by hand with no reporting of insurance write-offs. Prior to the purchase, I had no idea what to look for when purchasing an existing practice and how to determine if the information you are given is truthful or complete. Even if I had been given the correct information, I would not have known the meaning or the significance of it. So, I told patients that I wasn't a preferred provider on their PPO dental plan, and I didn't accept HMOs. That news combined with the fact that most of the dentistry this dentist had done needed to be redone was the perfect storm; most of the patients left my practice. Within one year, my newly purchased practice shrank to half its original size. I realized the money I had paid him wasn't for a thriving, profitable dental practice. It was for a very old, musky-scented office that had not seen a fresh layer of paint in thirty years with equipment belonging to a different century. I would have been better off starting out from nothing, and the money I paid this dentist would have been better spent on getting new patients and equipment. And I was disappointed to find that there was no manual or help available to figure out what to look for when purchasing a practice or how to make that practice profitable.

However, I had spent everything I had to get to this point. I was a business owner now and determined to succeed. Failing was not part of my DNA, so I pushed forward to become known in the community. I joined the chamber of commerce, toastmasters, the gym, and every association or organization that existed at that time, whether I shared their mission or not. I showed up for 7 a.m. breakfast meetings after working ten-hour days and used every membership as an opportunity to promote my practice. People wondered how I was able to be in so many places at once. I was determined to get to know people and let them know that I was the new dentist in town. I wanted them to remember my name and my office number if and when anything went wrong with their teeth.

My days were long. Besides patient care, I did the bookkeeping, paid the bills, wrote policies and job descriptions, complied with all the regulations, and a million other things. It was as if I was the bookkeeper, office manager, and hygienist. Sometimes, I even did the cleaning, sterilization, and operatory setup. The list goes on for miles. No job was beneath me. If something needed to be done and my assistant was out for lunch, I did it. By doing this, I got to know the operation of a dental practice from every angle.

For many years I didn't know why I was so emotionally drained and exhausted at the end of my days. It wasn't until much later that I realized this was because I felt all the emotions of my patients and employees. I'm an empath, which means I feel all the emotions, traumas, and negativity that everyone around me feels. There were no boundaries. I had no idea how to control this. Many of my patients, whether they knew it or not, were triggered just by entering my office. If they had negative experiences in the past, whether from events related to dentistry or not, they would be triggered. I would feel their negative emotions as though they were my own. If any of my employees came to work and were sad or frustrated because of something that happened in their personal life, I would feel the intensity of their sadness or frustration as though it was mine. As I absorbed and carried everyone else's negativities, I was drained until I had nothing left to give. This adversely affected my physical health in multiple ways. One example was intermittent headaches which, at first, although bothersome, were not of such intensity that rendered me incapable of ignoring them. For many years, I managed my stress by exercising five or six days a week doing aerobics and weight training. This kept me in shape, gave me flexibility and strength, and was a way for me to let go of steam. When I tore my hamstring and my knees could no longer tolerate heavy exercise, I was forced to change my exercise routine. My body was changing, and I had to adapt to those changes. Not knowing how to change, I resented and resisted the changes by doing what was familiar—working even harder than before. This is when I discovered that working any harder than I already was did not result in an increase in profitability.

You see, by this time, I had successfully grown my practice to become one of the best in the area and it was profitable. What was important to me was that I did not compromise patient care for profitability. Figuring how to do this was not easy. I made many mistakes, learned from them, and kept going, always pushing forward despite facing one adversity after another. In the following chapters, I will share how I reached this level of profitability, but right now I want to emphasize that profitability is not a state that once reached will repeat itself automatically each month. What worked once may not ever work again in the same way. It is smart to track and repeat those successful actions that brought you profitable periods, but keep in mind that the external conditions that existed during those periods may not remain the same. In business, nothing ever stays the same. Business by nature is not static. It is a living, breathing entity that is always in a state of flux. Toward the end of this chapter, you will see this in action when I describe the effects of external changes beyond my control on the profitability of my practice.

For a dentist, profitability alone is not impossible to achieve. In fact, many dentists will reach a certain level of profitability in their career on their own through trial and error and patience. It takes longer to achieve it this way, but it is doable. My business, like many others, had reached a certain level of success and profitability, but it had also reached a plateau and needed a different strategy. At the time, I didn't know what that involved.

It is worth mentioning again that the difficult and tricky part is not reaching profitability; it's maintaining and increasing it consistently, once it is reached. If you don't pay attention to the latter part of the previous sentence, you will lull yourself into a false sense of security that will crash in a moment's notice, much like waves in the ocean. As I will explain in this book, you will see how you can reach a consistent increase in profitability effectively by following the principles in each chapter.

Continuing the story, although I didn't know what would be involved in the new strategy of moving my practice beyond the plateau it had reached, one thing I did know was that I had to keep up with the changes in technology that were occurring with increasing speed in dentistry. I needed to incorporate digital x-rays, which required drilling holes in the walls. I knew that the age of the building had to be factored in, and I needed the landlord's help if my renovation revealed surprises behind the walls. After I asked for permission and help, my landlord started to give me a hard time. He told me he would rather let the place go empty than invest in a fresh layer of paint. In addition, instead of obtaining my permission, the landlord would enter my office suite during the weekends and do small jobs, leaving my office suite with two inches of dust and dirt as a surprise to be discovered Monday morning when I had to see patients. Trying to negotiate with him was like talking to a wall, so I decided to move instead of fight with my landlord. Finding a suitable location for and moving an established dental practice was not an easy task, but I was ready and knew it was necessary for me to continue practicing dentistry in accordance with my values. To my surprise, finding a location for a dental practice was mired with regulation after regulation. I was finally convinced to purchase instead of lease when I realized the cost of leasing square footage for a dental office is almost equal to purchasing it.

This catapulted me into a one-year project that, although exciting, required a village of expertise that I ended up spending a fortune on. The year I started this project, I unknowingly ended up with two full-time jobs. One was seeing patients and managing my existing dental practice; the other was planning for the new office, getting a real estate bank loan, hiring an architect, hiring a contractor, hiring an engineer, getting approval from the city at every juncture of the build-out, making sure the transition would be easy for my patients, trying to please my employees, and figuring out how to move everything and when to move to minimize hardship on everyone.

The problems with the move were plentiful and immensely stressful. It involved dealing with insurmountable overhead costs, managing patients and insurance companies, having the city delay permits, which meant we couldn't start seeing patients until two weeks after we moved, and so much more. I couldn't sleep. I was burning the candle at both ends.

Once completed, the build-out was beautiful, but I realized that despite all the planning, there would always be people who would not be pleased. Pleasing everyone in a task such as this was impossible. As dentists, we are trained to do our jobs well with a certain predictable outcome, but managing human beings and their negative feelings about change in a move such as this was anything other than a predictable outcome.

The year following the move brought a whole set of different problems. My body, which by now was worn out from having two full-time jobs for a year, was determined to get my full attention and let me know that the stress of being a dentist and a business owner could no longer be ignored. My headaches turned into migraines and their severity and duration increased. My keen and heightened awareness of everybody else's negative feelings and traumas was building up and weighing me down. Every day I became more and more aware that I needed to change the way I operated in order to maintain a profitable practice, but again and again, as certain as I became, I didn't know how or where to start.

When I first started practicing, technology wasn't as advanced as it is now. Keeping up with technological advancements meant a huge investment, involving the purchase of equipment, and training employees who were not so willing to embrace change. Many were in their mid-fifties and used to doing their job in a certain way; they were not selfless and had no reason to change. They didn't care that every day, new and better ways of doing things came to the forefront. Now that we had a computer and digital x-rays in each operatory and almost-paperless charts, with every glitch of the computer, my office came to a complete standstill (usually because somebody didn't turn off the computers properly at close-out the day before)—another aspect of the move I had not considered.

I realized very quickly that regardless of how well I plan things, there are always things that will go wrong. I could not apply the same principles of profitability that had worked well before to my changed circumstances and expect them to work. The overhead of the newly built office was ten times more than the old office and so were the number and complexity of problems. Another thing that I had no way of predicting was the 2007 financial crisis, which ushered in the 2008 Great Recession. Every day patients were calling to say they had lost their job—and their dental insurance. This wave of news was followed by the news that patients and their families were leaving California to go to another state. They came to my office to hug us one last time and we said our goodbyes. I felt deeply sad to see them go. These were patients who had been with me for decades, and I knew I would miss them. Once again, I lost half of my practice, but this time I felt I had also lost dear friends. My years of practicing selflessness and running myself ragged weren't doing me any good in the chaos life inevitably brings. Since I couldn't control everything, I had to find better ways of handling the chaos and becoming profitable again. At the same time, I also had to figure out how to stop absorbing everybody else's negative feelings. And then I had the dream.

Ever since childhood, I have had significant dreams. The feelings that ensued the day after the dream were intense and affected me for days afterward. Psychologists Krippner, Bogzaran, and De Carvalho (2002) have described some dreams as extraordinary when they are meaningful and anomalous, often impacting the dreamer's life in powerful ways.[1] One night, I truly discovered the validity of this statement. In my dream, I was in a rapidly flowing river and I could tell that the choice to be in this river in these circumstances was not mine. I was desperately looking for a branch of a tree or anything to grab so I could bring myself to safety, but there was nothing available. The river was flowing powerfully and rapidly, and my body was not strong enough to swim against the current. I had no way of getting myself to dry land. I was terrified by the realization that the river was in charge. Just when I thought things couldn't get worse, another fast-flowing and turbulent river joined the one I was in. Now there were two rivers flowing even more powerfully than before and my body was too weak and exhausted to get to safety. Again, just when I thought it couldn't get any worse, a third fast-flowing river joined forces with the two that I was in. At this point, I was being washed away against my will by the force of three joined rivers. As I was thinking that it really couldn't possibly get any worse, I realized I was rapidly approaching the edge of where the three rivers formed the largest waterfall I had ever seen. I was clearly in survival mode and not much was going through my mind except my prevailing death, which was turning into imminent death. I plummeted over the waterfall into the body of water below. I hit the surface and the weight of my body took me deep under the water. To my surprise, I didn't die. I stayed deep under the water, breathing, calm, and at peace. I no longer felt fear, resistance, or struggle, just harmony and unconditional

---

1   Krippner, Stanley, Fariba Bogzaran, and Carvalho André Pércia de. *Extraordinary Dreams and How to Work with Them*. Albany: State University of New York Press, 2002.

love. I felt that love and the peace through every cell of my being, so much so that I had no intention of moving toward the surface. I had survived in a form that was not possible to the rational mind or the scientific laws of the human body. But I had survived.

I woke up, sat on my bed in amazement, and went about my days wondering about the meaning of this dream for months.

At the time, I thought this dream was another validation that I was on the right path to finding a different way—a better way of practicing that did not involve sacrificing every aspect of myself to be a successful and profitable business owner. (I later realized that this dream had additional depth to its meaning, which I will discuss in Chapter 4.) At the time, this was enough validation for me to start my search with additional learning. After a thorough search, knowing that I would be giving up the little time off that I had on weekends, I threw myself back into school.

The education that was not available to me when I started practicing was now being taught as energy medicine and energy psychology. While I was still practicing and managing my business, I started a three-year certification that opened me to the world of knowledge that was exactly what I was looking for. In those three years, I also researched what I was learning on my own because I had to prove to myself that what I was learning really worked in a dental setting. To my surprise, not only were the results supportive, but I was never short of participants who were eager and willing to participate in the research. It was that education and those results that really turned the page for me. No longer was I convinced of a specific recipe for dental practice profitability that depended on immense self-sacrifice. I was learning to go with the flow, to accept that life—like the joined rivers—would take me in directions against my will, but if I could simply be and work with the river of life to plummet over the waterfall, it might just lead me to a place of peace and better understanding.

After two decades of not knowing how to alleviate the dental fears and anxieties of my patients, I found a way that alleviated those fears and anxieties without the use of pharmaceutical drugs. The details of The Fearless Way Method are in my first book, *The Well-Referred Dentist* (2020).[2] Alleviating the fears and anxieties of my patients was one of the first things that started bringing profitability back to my practice in a way filled with more joy than ever before.

Through also learning how to ground myself, I was no longer affected by everyone else's energies. By remaining centered regardless of what adversity came around the corner, I was able to maintain my energy, which positively affected everyone around me. By cleansing and balancing my chakras and releasing the hold that limiting beliefs had on me, a whole new vista of possibility opened up—both for me as a person and my practice's profits.

As I kept learning, I incorporated what I learned to help my patients get healthier. The results were astonishing. As I learned to keep my heart open without absorbing everyone's negative feelings, I was able to practice through the eyes of love. That single factor catapulted my practice forward into an entirely new level of success. It strengthened my relationships with my patients, and I was able to let go of those with whom I was not in alignment with love. My treatment plans were more geared

---

2   Saleh, Bita. The Well-Referred Dentist: The Essential Hidden Steps to a
     Profitable & Anxiety-Free Practice. New York: Morgan James Publishing,
     2020.

toward resolving the root problem instead of resolving the symptoms. Also, by incorporating The Fearless Way Method of alleviating patient's dental fears and anxieties, my treatment plan acceptance rates were better than ever.

By balancing my left and right brain, my efficiency increased. Through learning to meditate, my migraines slowly became less frequent and severe until they were completely gone. During this time, my boundaries became very clear and enforcing them without guilt became easier and easier.

As I watched my profits continue to increase from this new method of being, I came to understand what it really means to stop swimming against the flow of the river. Your body and mind can only swim against the river, fighting chaos with sacrifice and discipline, for so long. At some point, you have to accept that profitability can't be reached with a step-by-step plan for success and turn inward to find your individual path to profitability—with a few guiding principles that I want to share in this book. Everything that worked for me may not work exactly the same way for you, but with the principles I've learned, and sometimes the help of a coach, you can find your path to sustainable profitability. It starts by recognizing that within the chaos and loss of control in life, it is necessary to trust that the river always knows where it's taking you. Let's dive in!

Reflection Points:
1. Is profitability acquired by a state of "being" or "doing" or both?
2. Describe how you would need to be and what you would need to do to be profitable or to increase your profitability?

3. Are you currently as profitable as you want to be?
4. How would you know if you were compromising your values for profitability?
5. What are you not willing to compromise for profitability?

CHAPTER 3:

Create a Practice Where You are the Best Version of Yourself

When I started my practice, I didn't have a mentor or a consultant or a coach. In fact, I didn't have anyone like that for the first ten years of my career. I didn't even know what made someone a great or a good coach or consultant or mentor, nor were there books or resources that I could rely on to provide me with the valuable information I needed to navigate the landmines that my career as a single practitioner and business owner was about to unleash on me.

Now that I'm further along in my journey, I know it's imperative for you to know the difference between a coach and a consultant. The simplified difference between the two is the presence or absence of their expertise in your industry. A consultant is someone who is or has been a licensed dentist and has practiced dentistry while owning and operating their dental practice for, in my opinion, at least two decades. The reason I find it's important to have at least two decades of experience is because that is the only way they would understand the challenges that you are or will be facing in your business. They would have had to find the solution to those challenges themselves along their way to success.

A certified professional coach, however, is not required to have expertise in your profession. The way that each of these professionals work with you is different as well. Coaches are not required to provide solutions for you. With pure coaching, the answers come from the client and not the coach, as opposed to consultants who are experts in your field and can provide you with solutions, advice, and guidance. I typically recommend hiring a consultant in addition to a certified professional coach. The best option is to have the best of both worlds, which could also mean hiring a professional who is both a certified coach and a consultant. This person will know when to put their consultant hat on, like when you need to solve a problem head-on, and they will know when to put their coaching hat on, like when you need to learn to develop your leadership skills. In an ideal world, you would be hiring one person with the expertise to do both jobs.

For example, let's say you want to learn to ride a bicycle. A bicycle consultant is an expert who knows how to ride a bicycle, has two decades of experience riding bicycles herself, and knows all the reasons that a person can succeed or fail when learning to ride a bicycle. This bicycle consultant can write the best and most comprehensive instruction manual on how to learn to ride a bicycle successfully and quickly so you will possess all the instructions that you would need to learn to ride a bicycle. Therefore, a bicycle consultant is an expert in riding bicycles who can teach you the process or method of learning to ride a bicycle. A certified bicycle coach, on the other hand, walks beside you after you get on the bicycle and guides you through the process of learning until you're confident enough to do it on your own. A bicycle coach will not have the expertise to tell you how to avoid potholes or what to do when you hit one. They walk alongside you as you hit the pothole and then help you figure out how to get up and ride again.

To provide you with an example in dentistry, if a dentist is in a situation where they may not know whether someone in their office is embezzling from them but they have an inkling that something is off, a consultant will know exactly where to look, which reports to review, and how to find out how much money is missing and why and who the culprit is as quickly as is possible. They can also give you detailed instructions to implement policies that will prevent an incident such as this from occurring again. A consultant can help resolve this problem quickly and efficiently based on their significant knowledge, understanding, and experience from being a dentist who has owned and managed their own dental practice for over two decades. A coach will not be able to do any of this, but they could help you with the implementation of the consultant's instructions. A coach can help you develop the capacity to become the person who never allows this to happen in their office. They will be able to restore your confidence and inspire you to be a confident leader again. There are many other differences between a consultant and coach, such as fees charged, but for the sake of understanding the major differences between the two and how it impacts you and your practice, this is enough ground for you to understand the value of both. Therefore, finding an expert who is trained to do both consulting and coaching is extremely valuable for the owner of a dental practice.

Dentistry is not a profession that glorifies self-reflection; yet, what I have discovered is that without self-reflection, we lose the significance of why we do what we do. The expected culture in our profession is to put our chin up, grow some hair on our chest, and keep showing up and moving forward as every other dentist and business owner has done before us.

Although, somewhere along the way, most dentists will figure out how to gain a certain level of profitability—enough so they can stay in practice—most of the learning happens through trial and error at the price of their health. If you are reading this book, you are wiser than most because you know there must be an easier way to profitability than blindly trying to figure it out, self-sacrificing on your own.

I encourage you to start from the beginning and read the chapters in sequence all the way through at least once. After that, depending on where you are in your practice, you can revisit the chapters that interest you the most so that you can explore them in more depth. I include many different reflection points that serve as the foundation for looking inward to create a profitable practice. I hope that you will explore all of them, but if you decide not to, I would encourage you to reflect on why you wish to bypass them. If the answer is because you have never encountered a problem in that area, I would caution you to reconsider. Remember the rivers. Anything can happen at any moment without notice or warning in the life of a dental practice owner. If we only took action when an urgent need forces us into finding a solution, we would always be operating in a state of emergency. Our efforts would be primarily put toward putting fires out all day—a path that will not lead to profitability. This is similar to a patient who only comes to see you when they have an emergency. You might caution this patient that this is not any way to obtain or retain a state of dental health. In the same token, remember: The results you get will be directly proportional to how much time and effort you're willing to put in.

If you feel that this book will be useful to any of your friends or colleagues, make sure to share it with them. We are all members of a profession that we're proud of and we need to look after one another. We need to remember that competing is a behavior that should have ended when we completed our training. It needs to stay in the past.

My wish for you is that you learn the important lessons without unnecessary suffering and that you understand the path to profitability doesn't have to be a treacherous one. It doesn't have to include being hazed or bullied or sued by anyone who belongs to the 20 percent of the population that cause 80 percent of problems. Profitability does not have to be a cause of suffering, nor does it have to lead to burnout, illness, depression, addiction, early retirement, thoughts of suicide, or any array of problems.

I want you to know that this book has found its way into your hands for a reason. It's not by accident that you picked up this book. In whatever way these words have found their way to you, please know it wasn't a random event. You are meant to be reading these words. The knowledge and the lessons shared with you here about manifesting a consistently profitable practice can lead you to shift paths, guide you toward love, help you find joy, and maybe even save your life.

This is the book that should have been given to you at your dental school graduation. In it, I will share the main topics and principles relevant to having a consistently profitable practice so you can view the road to profitability as a clear path rather than one that includes puzzles to solve and roadblocks to overcome around every corner.

It is my sincere hope and expectation that by reading this book, you will have a clear understanding of how to become the type of person who can seamlessly rise above her limitations and fears and be inspired to become a leader who can lead her team consistently to profitability.

More specifically, this book will help you:

- Attain your profit targets consistently and with ease each year while balancing your overhead like a professional
- Increase treatment plan acceptance and maximize the help offered by insurance
- Attract high-value new patients, keep existing patients coming back, and love those you need to let go
- Decrease no-shows and last-minute cancellations
- Get paid in a timely manner for your expertise
- Own your power as a leader by choosing and retaining the right team members
- Prosper without losing your health and well-being in the process

The following paragraphs provide a more detailed summary of what you'll learn.

In Chapter 4, you will understand the foundation of profitability and how to win the profitability game without relinquishing your power to limiting negative thoughts.

In Chapter 5, you will get clear on who your authentic self is (voice/brand), what your values are, what is fulfilling for you, and what your sense of meaning and purpose is at work. As you clarify these, your boundaries will naturally fall into place and be clearly defined.

In Chapter 6, you will become very clear about who you are guided to serve.

In Chapter 7, you will discover the best ways to attract high-value new patients and how to elevate your patient care so your existing patients remain loyal and refer others.

In Chapter 8, you will determine if accepting insurance is right for your practice or not, and if it is, you will decide which ones to accept and which ones to reject. You will also know how to put systems in place so that insurance will not swallow all your resources and time.

In Chapter 9, you will see all the steps required to achieving your desired monthly and yearly production goals with an emphasis on high treatment plan acceptance rates.

In Chapter 10, you will create solid and clear collection policies so that monthly billing is no longer needed because your collection is 90 percent or more of production.

In Chapter 11, you will learn the difference between fixed and variable costs and how to keep overhead in check with the help of your team members.

In Chapter 12, you will discover how to find the right employees, how to build a team that is an extension of you, and how to let them go if boundaries are crossed while maintaining your power as the leader of your practice.

In Chapter 13, you will see the value of stopping and surrendering long enough to learn deeper lessons. In doing so, you will be able to repair energetic leaks that hinder or slow down your forward flow.

In Chapter 14, you will realize the importance of your mental, emotional, and physical health and that they're not negotiable. You will understand why this has to be prioritized for profitability to have a chance of materializing with consistency, regardless of how many curveballs life throws at you.

I'm grateful that you're here. No matter where you are in your practice, let's start at the beginning.

Reflection Points:

1. Who do you believe can help you the most in your practice: A Coach or a Consultant or a combination of both? Why?
2. What are three qualities of an effective leader?
3. Which qualities do you possess as a leader? Is there room for improvement?
4. What are three fears that keep repeating in your thoughts? How are they limiting you in your practice?
5. Describe three situations that cause you to react instead of lead?

CHAPTER 4:

See through the Eyes of Love

One of my patients, Jo, used to arrive at my office on his bicycle, wearing the same shirt and knee-length pants appointment after appointment regardless of the weather. Well, maybe it wasn't exactly the same outfit, but it was the same color and style each time. He always wore tennis shoes and had a properly trimmed beard that resembled Santa Claus's. He always paid cash, and he always complained about my fees with various grunting noises when he was asked to pay. Depending on the volume and intensity of his grunts, sometimes I wasn't sure if he would return. Jo was an introvert and didn't like to talk too much. Every time I spoke to him about his teeth during one of my many attempts to educate him, he looked at me as though I was crazy. I wasn't sure if he understood a word I was saying, but as his dentist, in a language I knew, I said what I had to say. According to the standard of care, I was required to educate my patients about the existing condition of their teeth, recommend treatment, and review their options along with the consequences of not following my recommendations. As you know, quality of patient care was very important to me, as was patient education. I couldn't understand why Jo never accepted my treatment plans when I explained every aspect so clearly.

Without realizing, I had formed my own conclusions about him based on what I knew as a twenty-six-year-old dentist and business owner, which was pretty limited. After a while, I started feeling like a robot, just repeating the same treatment plan over and over without expecting a different response from Jo. In fact, my renditions became faster and faster over time. He came for his checkups and cleanings, the occasional cavity was fixed, but he never reached the dental health that I knew was possible for him.

Jo is just one example of a wide array of patient personalities that I encountered every day. I was trained to be very organized, logical, precise, and detail-oriented. Throughout the nine years of my higher education, my left brain was carefully cultivated to dominate. I knew dentistry very well. I was a great practitioner, and my work, as long as patients took good care of their teeth and their restorations, rarely failed. As long as everything went according to plan, I had great success.

Does this sound familiar?

But life, especially as a doctor and business owner, rarely goes according to plan. I couldn't shake the feeling of having been reduced to a robot whose success depended upon the execution of a specific, practiced plan over and over again in a business where I was treating human beings whose lives also rarely ever went according to plan.

Although I didn't know it then, I needed to see my patients and my practice's profitability through the eyes of love instead. Another aspect that I needed to pay attention to was balancing the right and left sides of my brain. As you read the rest of this chapter, you will see the importance of seeing through the eyes of love and balancing the two hemispheres of your brain on the profitability of your practice.

Now, keep in mind this was in the early '90s when no one even knew, much less talked about, the importance of balancing the right and left hemispheres of the brain or what they each represented in the context of patient care. Knowing what I know now, I can see that my right brain was very dominant while I was growing up. I was creative and had the ability to visualize worlds within worlds of possibilities. I could write stories in so much detail that it was difficult to separate reality from imagination. It was a magical and colorful world that spilled into my dreams. As I mentioned earlier, these intense dreams would affect me for days afterward as they often foretold events that had not yet occurred or people I had not yet met. Most of my dreams were precognitive—the ones that foretold events— but I also had dreams belonging to other categories that I will explain later.

Another aspect that I had no control over was my ability to feel every emotion deeply without realizing that most of what I felt didn't belong to me. I didn't realize that I was an empath. Being an empath means feeling other people's feelings as though they are your own. This is the reason empaths often feel drained; they feel and absorb everyone else's feelings like a sponge. Empaths need alone time to recover as they slowly allow all the different feelings they have absorbed to seep out. Until they have let go of everyone else's feelings, they cannot know which ones are their own.

The emotions that resulted from my dreams and from being an empath created a lonely world for me. I was born into a family where being an empath and having dreams that came true were not embraced, although my father, a renowned and highly respected neurosurgeon, was my idol. I have always had the highest respect and unconditional love for my father. However, the one thing we never saw eye to eye on were dreams and their significant influence over my emotions and my life. He believed in "science" and only the science that he was taught while studying medicine. He did not know that there is also dream science or that being an empath is a real condition. My dreams and recollections of them only initiated countless hours of debate and discussion during which he explained the many reasons why dreams are nonsense and that the only logical way to deal with them is to casually dismiss them. Although his left brain dominated his thinking, my right brain dominated mine. I did not know how to deal with the heavy emotional impact and crippling loneliness that infected my days long after the dream had passed. I wished that I would not dream again and to not feel so deeply.

Through advancements in science, we now know that the right and left hemispheres of the human brain are responsible for different functions. The right brain is associated with creativity and is responsible for expressing emotions, perceiving facial signals, coordinating singing, comprehending music, reading body language, carrying out visual-spatial tasks needed to throw and catch a ball or ride a bike, and facilitating insight and intuitive reasoning. The right brain allows us to both literally and metaphorically understand the big picture and context because it processes things simultaneously rather than in sequence. For example, we can perceive a whole face at once instead of one feature at a time. Les Fehmi and Jim Robbins in their book *The*

Open-Focus Brain (2008) call this parallel processing.[3] The left brain, on the other hand, is the dominant hemisphere put to work in dental and medical school where students learn rigid, goal-oriented attitudes. It is responsible for a more objective, separate, and rational thinking. It governs language, speech, reading, writing, and processing information in a sequential or serial way, which includes such tasks as grammar, math, typing, and keeping score.

Much like either being right-handed or left-handed, people are known to have a dominant brain hemisphere. Many occupations, such as dentistry or medicine, favor and reward left-hemisphere dominance and marginalize those with right-hemisphere dominance. The result is a healthcare system that appears materially rich but is destitute in many significant ways. For humans to function at their best, equal attention must be given to the right and left hemispheres. As I'll explain in more detail later in the chapter, this is so important for patient care and the profitability of a dental practice.

In their book *Extraordinary Dreams and How to Work with Them*, psychologists Stanley Krippner, Fariba Bogzaran, and Andre Percia De Carvalho describe some dreams as extraordinary when they are meaningful and anomalous in nature, often impacting the dreamer's life in powerful ways. I discovered the validity of this statement in the previously mentioned three-river dream, along with many others, and also learned why I could not hold back my dreams even if I tried.

Before I discuss my three-river dream as an extraordinary dream, I want to point out that there are also ordinary dreams that

---

3   Fehmi, Les, and Jim Robbins. *The Open-Focus Brain: Harnessing the Power of Attention to Heal Mind and Body*. Boston, MA: Trumpeter, 2008.

can be useful in the life of the dreamer as well. People, including myself, often dream ordinary dreams that serve useful purposes such as consolidating memory, solving problems, downloading emotions, and planning for the future, just to name a few. Once the meaning of an ordinary dream is understood, you can take steps to figure out how to use the lessons of the dream to make your life better (Krippner and Ellis, 2009).[4]

Mostly, my extraordinary dreams belonged to five categories: clairvoyant, precognitive, spiritual and visitation, personal myths and problems, and lucid dreams. It is worth noting that nature knows no categories and it is mostly humans who make these categories. Hence, some dreams are bound to be combinations of the extraordinary categories with overlap. My three-river dream was an example of an extraordinary dream that shed light on my personal myths and personal problems.

According to Krippner et al. (2002), personal myths are woven from many different strands, one of which includes the events of the past.[5] Often these dysfunctional myths lead to the creation of personal problems pertaining to, for example, work issues and finances. In my case, the theme of lack of safety seemed to prevail. As I wrote in Chapter 2, I moved my practice to a different location after eighteen years of being in the same location and spent a fortune building this office space to capture the essence of how I practiced dentistry. That move came with lots of changes that disrupted my regularly scheduled programming.

Krippner et al. (2002) wrote that, according to Montague Ullman, dreams are similar to corrective lenses. Like corrective

---

4   Krippner, Stanley, and Debbie Joffie-Ellis. *Perchance to Dream: The Frontiers of Dream Psychology.* New York: Nova Science Publishers, Inc., 2009.
5   Ibid.

lenses, if we learn to use our dreams properly, we are able to "see ourselves and the world about us with less distortion and with greater accuracy" (158). Krippner et al. (2002) explained that as a person matures throughout their lifetime, personal mythologies also mature. A person may experience a mythic crisis, which represents a conflict in a person's personal mythology affecting her feelings, thoughts, or behaviors. This mythic crisis occurs when an ongoing personal myth becomes so outdated or dysfunctional that the psyche generates a counter-myth to organize perceptions and responses in a different way. The greater the conflict, the more intensely the effects of the dream are felt and the greater the impact on the individual. In working with dreams, Krippner et al. (2002) suggested paying attention to the "feeling tone" (160) of the dream in terms of energy and vitality. [6] Although the feeling tone is dependent on the dreamer's style of thinking and feeling, the following explanation sheds some light on the dream's feeling gauge. They wrote, "'Old myth' dreams typically feel defeating, hopeless, and draining in terms of energy and vitality. 'Counter myth' dreams typically tend to feel hopeful, optimistic, even exhilarating. 'Integration' dreams tend to produce a calm, positive, realistic feeling." (160)[7]

Therefore, it is helpful to give importance to the feeling tone of the dream rather than the minute details. This type of dream (personal myths and problems) contains enormous healing capacity for the dreamer if understood properly. For me, this personal myths and problems dream fell into the subcategory of an "integration" dream, because the feelings that ensued

6   Ibid.
7   Ibid.

while I was dreaming where, at first, defeating, draining, and hopeless as I was being carried against my wish down the river (old myth) and then turned into hope and exhilaration as I was able to survive, breathe, and feel unconditional love under the water (counter-myth). Upon awakening, my feelings were ones of peace, hope, and calm. I had no doubt that this dream had a profound meaning and message for me. In this dream, the old myth ("you are always alone and unsafe") combined with the counter-myth ("you are never alone and are always safe") produced a new myth. The new myth was that there can be safety, support, and fulfillment even when I have no control of the chaos pulling me under the water.

We're all individuals with a past and varying backgrounds, but we also all have a common thread: We have all finished the arduous task of completing dental school. Although our training has prepared us extremely well as dental practitioners, when we step into the role of a business owner, we are inevitably stepping into a leadership role that we're not trained for. Whether you have a small office with one employee or a large office with a team, the fact remains that you're a human being who carries with her the wounds and myths of her past that will eventually get in the way of your success and profitability. Life will throw anything that you have not resolved at you in a thousand different ways until you resolve it. For me, life showed me over and over again that what I thought I needed to feel safe was only an illusion.

When I viewed myself as different from my patients, like I did with Jo, those feelings of individuality only led to separation and judgment. I was solely accessing my left brain to define who I was and who I thought he was. According to my cultivated dominant left brain, as opposed to the dominant right brain in my childhood, I was a highly educated, intelligent single adult female in her mid-twenties who worked hard, was selfless, and was willing to sacrifice herself and her personal life to succeed in her business. I persevered through difficulties without showing my emotions and continually showed up every day ready to work harder than the day before. Although a lot of this was true, it wasn't the entire truth about me, the same way that what I saw in Jo was not the entire truth about him.

What usually separates humans from each other is our attachment to our stories and the illusion of our individuality, which allows our ego to become the source of our pain and suffering. This was my reality and my story ... until I realized that love could tell a different story.

In *Power vs. Force*, David Hawkins (1995) a well-known psychiatrist and physician, wrote about his extensive research whereby, using kinesiology and muscle testing, he was able to define a range of values for the energy fields of human consciousness and their emotional correlates.[8] The levels ranged from one to 1,000, and 200 was used as the decisive level at which force and power were divided. It was determined that all levels below 200 are destructive in the life of the individual, as well as society, and levels above 200 are constructive expressions of power. Shame has an energy level of twenty and grief has an energy level of seventy-five. Fear is at energy level one hundred, anger is at 150, and courage has energy level of 200. For example, if you or your team members are at energy levels below 200 (shame, guilt, apathy, grief, fear, desire, anger, and pride), you are considered destructive to yourself and/or

---

8   Hawkins, David R. Power vs. Force: The Hidden Determinants of Human Behavior. West Sedona, AZ: Veritas Publishing, 1995.

your patients. Love, however, has an energy level of 500. Love in this context is not what is often described by the mass media, which focuses on love in the realm of sexuality and desire. The love described here is unconditional, unfluctuating, permanent love that is not dependent on external factors. Love as a state of being is forgiving, nurturing, and a supportive way of relating to the world. This love emanates from the heart. It is not intellectual because it doesn't emanate from the mind. You can't think yourself into this state of being. This love is so pure in its motive that it has the ability to lift others up and accomplish great things. There is no separation between people at this level of love. This love focuses on understanding our oneness and removes barriers to connection. When dentists, physicians, and other healthcare providers operate at this level of love, they can make a significant difference in the lives of their patients by facilitating true healing at the source of disease rather than just resolving the symptoms. Patients respond to this kind of love. They are more likely to continue coming to your practice and accepting your treatment plans when they experience that level of connection upon entering your office. This, in turn, leads to a more profitable practice.

When I saw Jo through the eyes of love, I no longer judged him or was afraid to connect with him. Seeing through the eyes of love enabled me to synchronously give attention to both hemispheres of my brain, which then allowed fluid communication among the different regions of my brain. I was able to effortlessly and naturally look him in the eye and ask him what, if anything, was important to him. To my surprise, he said, "My health." That was the beginning of an effective doctor–patient relationship in which I was able to explain how he could achieve good dental health—in his language. It turns out that

Jo could afford the moon and the sun for his health. He only rode his bicycle because it was good for his health, and he wore what he wore because he didn't believe style was a necessity. He thought it was a waste. But his health was important, and he didn't grunt when he paid for a huge treatment plan because now he understood that it was for his health.

If you have pets, you know what seeing through the eyes of love looks like better than words can explain. It is the kind of love I saw every day in the eyes of my beloved dog, Pumpkin, who accompanied me to my office and taught me the unconditional and uncomplicated nature of love. He gave me the gift of seeing what it meant to truly see through the eyes of love. I'm inviting you to see your practice and your patients through the eyes of this kind of love for the rest of your days. In any situation that arises, before determining what action you will take, reflect on one question: "What would love say?"

Reflection Points

1. Write three short stories about yourself that best describe who you are as: i) a person; ii) a dentist; and iii) a business owner.

2. Reflect on each story and write an answer to: "What would love say about the person who wrote each story?"

3. Choose one fear that is present right now. After identifying the fear, get angry at this fear and then use courage to face it. By doing so, you will slowly raise your energy level from fear (energy level one hundred) in small increments (anger and courage) to finally access love (energy level 500), which can hold the fear tenderly and move it through and out of your body. When fear is removed, space will open up for you to stand in your

power. This is how you can begin creating the habit of seeing your patients through the eyes of love instead of seeing a series of problems throughout the day. Keep in mind the importance of doing this slowly. When a patient is experiencing fear or anxiety, if you or your assistant try to comfort and encourage them by saying things like "It won't hurt," "You'll be fine," "It's all in your head, it's not real," "It's a quick procedure and will be over before you know it", or try to distract them by telling a joke, the difference in energy levels will be too high and the patient will not be able to relate to you. They will leave your practice believing that you're not the dentist for them.

CHAPTER 5:

You Are Your Practice

When a patient leaves our practice, it's upsetting. Because, as dentists, we're highly responsible, we question everything and wonder if we could have done better to prevent the patient leaving. Even if we're glad that the patient left, there is always some negative emotion attached to this event. While you are typically the reason patients walk in the door, you are not always the reason they leave.

Based on my experience of practicing for thirty years and moving my office location once, I have found that in terms of loyalty, there are three types of patients in a dental practice. The first type is loyal to the doctor. They will follow you wherever you go, within reason, and don't care if you accept their insurance or not. They're responsible and show up for their appointments and pay your fees without complaining. They have many of the traits of your ideal patient. The second type are loyal to the location of your office. One could also say that they're loyal to the neighborhood or the town. If you move out of that zip code, it doesn't matter if you moved as little as five or as many as ninety miles away because they will drop you like a hot potato. Their list of reasons is usually long and convoluted. Some may actually tell you the truth, which is that they're loyal to the town and not you, or, if they want to spare your feelings, they will say, "I don't drive on the freeway," or "I hit too much traffic going that way," and on and on. The third type of patient is loyal to their insurance. They may appreciate and respect you, but if you're no longer a preferred provider on their insurance, they will find someone who is because the only thing that matters to them is how much they pay out of pocket.

Knowing that these are the types of patients available for you to treat, the natural next step would be defining which type of patient you want in your practice. As most of my consulting and coaching clients do, we all want to have our practice filled with the first type: loyal to the doctor. However, I would like to invite you to reflect on who you are or who you want to be before answering. If you've never done this, you may find it to be a very simple question at first, but upon reflection, most find that it's anything but simple. You might start out saying, "I want to help patients and be profitable," but soon you'll find that there are many variables attached to this one simple sentence. You will most likely soon give up because you realize the complexity of the task requires many considerations and you may say you'll do this another day when you have more time to dedicate to it but that day will never come because it will always feel like an endless task.

Why is it a good idea to start with this? Why don't we skip it for now? Why don't we just figure out how to get more new patients? These are the varying questions I hear from my clients when they first start working with me. And here's the answer:

Without knowing who you are, the rest of your business will be a guessing game. You will be at the mercy of the circumstances that you have no control over, and, instead of leading, you will be reacting. You will be frustrated, and, after a while, you might wonder why you're not able to be more profitable when you're working so hard.

One reason it feels cumbersome to reflect on who you are is because, as a human being with a business, your thoughts are many and wide in range. It's imperative to settle the many thoughts that you have going around in your head before doing this exercise, and the best way to do that is by grounding.

Grounding is a practice that connects your body to the earth and allows you to be in the present moment, creating a state of physical and emotional balance. Negative thoughts, emotions, and beliefs can result in stress and have an adverse effect on the body and how we show up for our patients. When your internal world is filled with negative thoughts and feelings and your mind is racing with frustration, that is who you're being: a very stressed-out and frustrated doctor. That is how your patients are seeing you, as someone who can't possibly help them. When properly grounded, it's possible to experience the same level of peace and unconditional love that I wrote about when I was under the water in my three-river dream.

In *The Power of Now*, Eckhart Tolle (1999) wrote about the value of being present in the moment by not allowing your mind and fearful thoughts about the future, negative memories, and incidents from the past to mar the experience of the present moment[9]. When properly grounded, your energy will vibrate at

---

9   Tolle, Eckhart. *The Power of Now: A Guide to Spiritual Enlightenment.* Novato, CA: New World Library, 1999.

a higher level, and, based on entrainment, this will allow your team members and patients to do the same. Entrainment in this context refers to a natural phenomenon that occurs wherein an entity with a lower frequency of vibration when placed in the presence of another entity with a higher vibration responds synchronously by increasing its energetic vibration to match the other entity's dominant higher vibrational frequency. Please go to my website www.drbitasaleh.com to request the link to a grounding meditation.

Let's look at an example of grounding in practice and the result. For years, every December in my office, there seemed to exist an unwanted crazy energy: fast and aberrant. Patients came in frazzled from the hectic looming of the upcoming holidays, drivers were speeding and cutting each other off, and there was an uninvited busyness all around. This affected my patients, my team, and me. One day during this busy time, my assistant made a rookie mistake that affected my work and I ended up having to redo what I was doing and ran late. I quickly took note that although this incident was upsetting, it would be handled best if I approached it from a grounded state. Usually going through a grounding exercise takes at least ten minutes, but once you are properly trained, you can visualize an image of your grounded state and instantly be in that state. By feeling grounded and at peace, I was able to prevent my energy from going down into frustration, so when I spoke to her about her mistake, she was able to understand how to prevent it from happening again instead of feeling that she had failed. She was able to maintain her energy at the same level as my grounded state and we were able to get through our day without transferring unnecessary stress to each other, other team members, or our patients.

When you are in a grounded state, you will have a clear mind and feel more connected to yourself and your values. To uncover your values, think of a moment or an experience that you cherish and treasure. As you recall the details of this experience, you will realize what aspects made this experience fulfilling for you. Perhaps it was a feeling of deep connection. If this resonates, you may conclude that having deep connections is a value for you. Values determine who we are as individuals with our own unique essence. Our values allow us to be true to ourselves, make priorities, and know what is important to us— what we cannot compromise.

Consider two dentists who have different values about running on time. The one who doesn't value it will run late, has no problem making patients wait, and is fine with patients showing up late since it doesn't make her feel pressured. The second dentist who values being on time goes through a great deal of planning to make sure she schedules her patients in a way that means no one has to wait. When an emergency makes her run late, she makes sure that the next patient gets adequate notice and an apology. In the same token, if one of her patients shows up late, she gets upset because she will be running late for the rest of the day.

Knowing your values becomes important when you set up policies in your practice. In the first dentist's office in this scenario, their policy is to see patients when they arrive late without consideration given to anyone else, including the next patient who now has to wait. In the second dentist's office, they may have a policy to design an alliance with patients who show up late once and, if they continue to be late, they are dismissed from the practice. Since the policy is in place and all team members are aware and know how to design an alliance with the patient who consistently shows up late, the patient's incidents of lateness will be minimized because they have been notified consistently over time. So, the office will run smoothly for this dentist. If, however, a patient disregards the notices, there will be no angst or doubt when the dentist dismisses this patient because the dentist will know that she values her time and that of her other patients more than she values the business from that one patient. The income she loses by dismissing this patient will be recovered exponentially by other patients who honor and respect her value of being on time.

Defining values and setting policies that respect those values will help you put your boundaries in place much easier than if you don't know what your values are or have not defined them. Clearly defined values, policies, and boundaries also allow you to feel fulfilled and happy instead of viewing your office as a place where no one listens to you, everything is chaotic, and no one takes you seriously when you try to enforce policies.

In the previous chapter, we talked about seeing your practice and patients through the eyes of love; however, you must see yourself through the eyes of love before you can see others that way. The second dentist mentioned above cannot possibly feel love for the patient who consistently shows up late. No one can see someone else through the eyes of love when resentment is what they feel first. It's important to note that you actually can be loving by letting this patient go so that they can find a dentist who is willing to treat them regardless of their chronic lateness. It's wise to recognize that as long as a patient is under your care, you are required to hold certain boundaries that allow you to treat them through the eyes of love and nothing else. Therefore, if resentment or another negative feeling peeks in, you know there is a value that is not being honored by that patient.

As part of defining your values and what you find to be fulfilling, I would like to invite you to also reflect on who you want to be at work. Your work life is a substantial part of your life. As a dentist and business owner, you are most likely treating patients anywhere from thirty-two to forty hours a week with at least another eight to twelve hours spent attending continuing education classes or other trainings and, of course, there is time spent on various aspects of running a business.

To illustrate discovering who you want to be at work, let's look at one of my clients. This client shared that she valued feeling calm throughout her workday more than any other feeling. We reviewed all of the aspects of her job that were stressful and found that the one area that stressed her out the most was being double-booked at the end of the day. She ended her days at 5 p.m. because she had to pick up her son from daycare. If she was late, she had to pay heavy fines to the daycare facility and, as a result, would be so stressed that she wouldn't be able to enjoy the time she had with her son in the evenings. Her patients were adult professionals who depended on their dental insurance premiums being paid by their employer. Every day starting at 3:30 p.m., her office phone would start ringing with requests from patients who needed to be seen after they ended their work for the day. Her receptionist would fit them in because they needed the production from those patients for the practice to meet its goals. We decided that spending time with her son was not negotiable and neither was staying calm throughout the day. The problem was that the patients who needed to be seen after-hours were the source of most of her production and she could not hire an associate to work in the evenings because she was not at a place in her practice where she could afford to do that. Therefore, fulfillment for her meant being able to meet her production goals (doing) while staying calm (being) throughout the day.

If she continued to treat patients who were double-booked at the end of her day, she would not be able to stay calm, and if she didn't treat them, she would not meet her production goals. She felt as though she was facing a double-edged sword. Had I not spent time at the beginning of our time discovering her values, her boundaries, and what she found fulfilling in her life, I would have found many solutions—none of which would have been the right ones for her. Having clarity was crucial to finding her an excellent short-term solution long enough that she could re-structure her practice to attract patients who fit her needs. When she came to me for help, she was ready to leave her practice and become a stay-at-home mom because of her frustration, and she would have resented her decision forever. However, by asking for help, she was able to find the right short-term solution within two weeks. Within twelve months, she had become consistently profitable without being double-booked or having to work after 5 p.m. ever again. The details of her solution are not relevant given the fact that that each person is different. The solution that worked for her may not work for someone else, even if they are facing the same circumstances.

A discussion of who you are would not be complete without paying attention to your negative thoughts, which occupy everyone's minds and direct our actions every day. Negative thoughts are as plentiful as they are varied. A few examples include thoughts centered around: a fear of failure, the unknown, not being good enough, scarcity, failing, and even success. The mind is incredibly good at what it does, and one of the things that it does exceptionally well is remember all the things that have threatened your survival in the past, regardless of whether they were due to perceived or real danger. The mind wants to keep everything the same so that we don't venture out of our comfort zone. Our minds can't distinguish that something that hurt us when we were a child cannot hurt us during adulthood. Thoughts that play over and over again in our minds become beliefs, and they can be limiting when they stop us from advancing and moving forward. The continual presence of these limiting thoughts brings forth a cascade of negative feelings, which in turn affect our mood and how we present ourselves to patients.

In the previous chapter, I said that what we don't resolve, life will throw at us over and over again until we resolve it. Don is a great example of this. Don had been a patient of mine for at least three years, and he always made his appointments at 7:30 a.m. because he had to be at work by 9 a.m. He was the first patient of the day for me. Don had several front upper teeth that were worn and contained old, discolored composite fillings. After a detailed exam and x-rays, his options were discussed with him and he chose to do porcelain veneers; six of his upper teeth were restored. Prior to and after cementation of the veneers, Don was very happy with the treatment. Even when I called him later that evening to check on him, his satisfaction had not waned. He had no sensitivity, and he was ecstatic with his new smile. Two weeks later, he called my office complaining about the veneers and was scheduled for a consult the next day at 7:30 a.m., as usual.

When I stepped into the operatory the next day promptly at 7:30 a.m., Don was seated in the dental chair and ready for attack. I felt like I was walking into enemy territory where you know land mines are present, but you have no clue about their location. His objective that day was not to share his dissatisfaction or to get my professional opinion. His objective was to land as many assaults as he could and walk away knowing that he had sufficiently destroyed his target, which was me. He didn't respond to my "good morning" and proceeded to tell me how unhappy he was with the veneers and that he wished he had never done them, amongst other words. I managed to convince him to let me examine his teeth and take x-rays. When I found nothing wrong with the treatment, he got up from the chair, threw his patient napkin on the floor, and asked for his records to be handed to him as he stormed out of my office.

I was shocked and had no idea how and why someone would behave like that. Even though I knew there was nothing wrong with the dentistry I had completed, this incident shook me and ruined my entire day, evening, and most of the following day. Dentists are trained to be perfectionists, and I was no different. The fear of not being good enough was a fear that always loomed over my head, especially in the first five years of my practice. I had no idea what I could have done to prevent this incident from occurring. My intuition told me that I didn't have all the information, but then again, how could I have all the information when my patient wanted to attack me instead of speak to me? Many years passed. Then one day as I was walking to the front of my office, I heard a familiar and insistent voice coming from the front asking my receptionist if I was in. As soon as I heard that voice, I had a strong feeling that it was Don, but I had no idea why he was there.

As soon as I got to the front, I saw that it was indeed him. He asked, "Dr. Saleh, do you remember me?" With utter surprise I thought to myself, "How could I not?" but instead I said, "Of course I do." In front of my receptionist and a few other patients in the waiting area, he said, "I came to say how sorry I am about how badly I behaved the last time I was here. That had nothing to do with you or the work you did for me. You in no way deserved that. Since then I have been to AA and I've been sober for a number of years. I'm here to ask for your forgiveness and to also find out if you'll take me back as a patient because I would really like to have you as my dentist again, but in no way do you need to agree. By the way, my veneers are doing very well even after all these years."

As healthcare professionals, we love to help our patients, so how could I refuse an apology like that? Don became a patient again, and our doctor–patient relationship was restored with no further upsets. He never again argued with me about my treatment recommendations or his out-of-pocket expense, and we both had an understanding that was centered around mutual respect and trust. I respected him for the courage it took to show up at my office and apologize to me when he could have just gone to another dentist.

Before I knew the reason why Don behaved the way he did that day, for the longest time I tried to understand the lesson inherent in this incident. I considered that perhaps if I had more confidence as a young doctor, maybe my energy would have been higher than his and instead of verbally attacking me, he would have found someone else who matched his low energy to download his anger on. This is an example of how the universe brings the lessons we need over and over until we learn them. Negative beliefs such as "not being good enough" carry a low vibrational frequency. Since low energy attracts low energy, perhaps that was the reason this patient chose me that day instead of someone else. I will never know if this would have played out the way it did if he was being treated by a more confident dentist, because confidence carries a higher energy than fear of not being good enough does. However, this experience taught me not to doubt myself. By no longer being in that lower-energy level, similar experiences have failed to affect me and my self-esteem since then. The lesson I learned was that negative beliefs are followed by negative feelings, which in turn give more power to those negative beliefs. Love, however, has a higher vibration than fear, so love and fear can never coexist.

The profession of dentistry calls for a lot from those who pursue it because it takes a lot of work, dedication, and investments of time and resources to become a dentist. It is by no means an easy profession. We not only have to keep up with advancements in dentistry, managing our business, endless regulations, and managing our patients, but we also have to take care of ourselves. Sometimes there is not enough time in a day to do all that. However, without taking care of ourselves, we cannot take care of the other aspects of our lives, at least not in the long run, including the profitability of our practice.

You are your practice. Learn to ground yourself at all times to the earth. Identify and define your values and know why what you have defined is a value. Know your boundaries, name your negative beliefs, and find ways to prevent them from running you and your life, including your business. Reflect every day on what is fulfilling for you. Ask yourself the big, powerful questions, such as: "What is my sense of meaning and purpose at work?" When you know your values, it's much simpler to reflect on your boundaries and the answers to deeper questions become clearer. Questions you can ask yourself are:

- Why, where, and when do I give myself permission to not honor myself?

- In what circumstances or to whom do I give my power away?
- Which boundaries do I need to hold to create space for my patients and honor their health?
- What am I not willing to risk?

Remember to start every day with being grounded in the present moment and keep reflecting on the big questions. Know that you can choose at any moment. You can choose to view your practice, your patients, and your employees through the eyes of love instead of fear and ask, "What would love say?"

Reflection Points

1. After you have grounded yourself properly, define who you are and who you want to be.
2. Identify at least three of your values.
3. Explain why these are values for you.
4. Define at least three boundaries by reflecting on what are you not willing to compromise.
5. Write at least three policies to support your values and boundaries.

CHAPTER 6:

Who are You Guided to Serve?

When you can't meet the demands of a patient because it goes against your values and boundaries, seeing the situation through the eyes of love can also mean loving that patient enough to let them go.

At first, it's natural to want to serve everyone. If your door has opened, you will want to keep it open. In your mind, that means working hard at every hour of every day. As long as you have patients, you will survive; at least, that is what you tell yourself. You will sign up for all the PPOs and maybe HMOs. Whatever you decide to do will be driven by wanting to get as many people (seeking dental treatment), through your door as possible. There is nothing wrong with this strategy as long as you're clear about your values and understand the consequences of each decision, but you won't know what your values are if you haven't taken the time to define them or haven't traveled down the road of practicing dentistry from the viewpoint of a business owner before.

If someone had asked me when I was twenty-five years old who my ideal patient was, I would have said, "A warm body who walks in through my door and is willing and able to pay me to fix their teeth or lack thereof." It was very simple and very general. Most recent graduates just want to perform beautiful dentistry and be their own boss. It's not very complicated.

The reality is that if you want to be your own boss and have a business, you will be called to do a lot more than just dentistry. You will need at least one employee when you start, and you will need to bring in new patients. Employees will be discussed in more detail in Chapter 12. For now, we'll discuss why it's important to identify who your ideal patient is.

You might wonder why I am asking you to limit yourself in such a way when you can help so many people. You have been trained in pediatric dentistry, endodontics, implants, restorative, periodontics, and maybe even oral surgery. You can do so much! But the reason I ask you to do this is because now that you're practicing, your health and energy in the long run are the most important assets that you need to protect. You might argue that you need to make a lot of money because you have student loans and other debt as well as overhead. I agree; you do need to make a lot of money. I would also argue that there are two ways of making money. One is the hard way, and one is the easier, more efficient way. I also would encourage you to spend the first five years of your practice treating everyone of all ages and performing every procedure allowed under your licensure so you can personally experience what that is like. That might be the only way for you to appreciate what I'm about to recommend.

Through performing a slew of different procedures, you will realize that there are certain procedures you enjoy doing and some that you don't. You might be good at some procedures, but you don't enjoy them that much. You will also realize there are some age groups that you enjoy and some that you don't. You will learn that one of the most important aspects of managing your dental practice is the speed at which you and your office can deliver excellent dentistry for a patient. This is one of the foundations of success. Your office needs to run efficiently whether you have one patient on your schedule for the morning or ten. To be efficient, your office needs to have the appropriate equipment, supplies, staff, and expertise. The simpler you keep everything, the easier it is to operate at this level. To do this, it's important to be very clear about who you are serving. To get really clear about this, imagine one ideal patient you would like to serve. Who would that be? What age are they? What is their profession? Do they go to movies? What are their hobbies? What do they read? How late do they like to stay up at night? Are they a morning person or a night owl?

If you had five pages to describe this one person in detail, how would you describe them? What are the values they honor? Why is this particular person your ideal patient? The clearer you are about this one person, the better. To illustrate, we'll take a look at two different dentists with two different ideal patients: dentist A and dentist B. These two dentists' ideal patients illustrate how these two dentists will have different practices based on who they are serving.

Dentist A's ideal patient is Sara, a thirty-year-old stay-at-home mom who is married with at least two children between the ages of two and nine. Dentist B's ideal patient is Cary, a single, fifty-year-old professional who is an executive or business owner. As you might imagine, Sara and Cary have very different needs when it comes to their availability, needs, and other factors.

Sara wants a dentist close to her home and to her kids' school. She wants a dentist who will treat her children, as well as herself and her husband, and preferably will offer financing and accepts the insurance offered at her husband's work. If a family discount is offered, that would be even better because she brings in three patients (her husband and her two children) in addition to herself. She wants to come in late afternoons when her kids are out of school and so does her husband because he works until 5 p.m. every day. Saturday hours would be even more convenient. She is involved with the PTA and is willing to refer other moms like herself to the practice if her family is treated well and likes the office. Out-of-pocket expense needs to be minimum because Sara's family is paying for four people and can potentially refer more. If any of them run out of insurance for the year, they prefer to postpone pending treatment (including cleanings and exams) to the following year when their insurance starts again. Even if a tooth is fractured and needs a crown, they will ask you to patch it up until their insurance benefits start again the following year.

Cary has different needs. She works long hours, so she needs early morning appointment times. She has insurance and an HSA account. However, if she cracks and loses a tooth, she will immediately opt in for an implant for replacement. Her appearance is very important to her so she will be interested in cosmetic procedures such as whitening and porcelain veneers. Her time is important too, so she wants a very efficient office where she can be in and out. She doesn't need financing because she has that covered with her credit cards that have high credit lines and give her rewards for every dollar spent. She wants the best treatment that dentistry has to offer and wants that treatment to last. She gets very irritated when she has to wait and wants to be seen on time every time she comes in. She shops at Louis Vuitton and Chanel and takes vacation at the top spas for her rest and relaxation. She has a personal trainer and a VIP gym membership.

Sara and Cary, although both females, have vastly different needs and wants. Your ideal patient will determine your office hours, the type of financing you offer, the staff you hire, the procedures you offer, the length of appointments, the advertising and marketing you spend your hard-earned dollars on, your policies, and so much more.

Sara wants late afternoon appointments whereas Cary wants early morning appointment times. The question then becomes: When do you prefer to work? When is your best time? I was an early bird. For many years, I offered 7:30 a.m. appointments because mornings were my best time, and I ended the day before it was dark. Having daylight hours available at the end of my day was important to me. As a result, I attracted the professionals who needed early morning appointments. For a while, I offered late afternoon hours one day a week, and I resented every patient appointment offered after 5:00 p.m. I finally accepted that offering late afternoon hours was not working for me. Every time a new patient called and requested late afternoon hours, I questioned whether I was doing the right thing by not offering them what they wanted. But I had also learned that many of the patients requesting late hours either would not show up or were not my ideal patients in one sense or another.

Your office hours also affect the employees you hire. I once hired a receptionist who was in her twenties and very eager to start. After a few months, it got harder for her to show up at 7:30 a.m. She started asking my other employees if I would be open to her starting at 9:30 or 10:00 a.m. and compensating by staying late. In addition to working at my office, she was also the manager of a band, and the band often played into early morning hours, which meant she couldn't get any sleep if she had to show up at my office ready for work at 7:30 a.m. If my values were not fully identified and clear, I might give this person a chance and agree to her determining her own work hours, which sends the wrong message to the rest of my employees who then need to compensate when she's not there. Soon, everyone will want to determine their own hours. By not being clear on your values and ideal patients, you can create an avalanche of problems for yourself and your practice.

Sara and Cary have different financial needs as well. Sara will want CareCredit with twelve months of free interest, which means you will have to write off 5 percent of the amount that she finances through you. This 5-percent write-off is in addition to the 60 percent write-off you are giving her because you are a preferred provider for the PPO insurance plan that she has through her husband's employer. With Sara, you may have to agree to wait until insurance pays their portion before she pays her co-pay unenthusiastically. She may even ask you to accept what insurance pays as full pay, which is illegal. She might even threaten to leave your practice along with her family because Dr. Smith down the street does do that. (Situations like this will be discussed in more detail in Chapter 8.)

Cary, however, is not interested in CareCredit because she would rather use her credit card that gives her rewards or pay you by check. With Cary, you will get to charge your usual, customary, and reasonable (UCR) fees. You will only pay your credit card merchant 2.5 percent of what you collected from her and if she pays you by check, you will not lose any money from what she has paid. She will pay you on the day of service because she hates getting bills in the mail since she considers that an inefficient use of her time.

As you can see, each patient will require different financial policies. If you try to serve everyone, you're entertaining a wide variety of financial needs so overwhelming that you may decide to not have a financial policy at all. None of your team members will know what to enforce, so your receivables will be sky high and you'll have cash flow problems. In addition, patients with balances will not be pleased when they get notices in the mail requesting payment. It might be more accurate to say that you have no financial policies if you decide on a per-case basis what to collect at the time of service and figure the rest out later. This is madness at best because collecting money from a patient who has already completed their treatment is a lot harder. In addition, you will soon resent the mounting receivable amounts, because you have bills, overhead, employee salaries, and yourself to pay. There is no green dollar tree that will magically pay your bills every month. If you don't have clear financial policies that lead patients to pay you in a timely manner, you will soon be in the red, stressed and resentful. Your financial policy will also determine the type of person you hire for your front office. I once had someone apply for a front office position who had recently declared bankruptcy. Although she was very presentable and experienced, declaring bankruptcy made her unsuitable for a role that included collecting money, so I had to pass on her. I had another front office employee who, after months of her working in my office, I found resented minors with parents who paid for their dental work. She was rude to these patients, but she couldn't see it. She later shared with me that she considered kids like that ungrateful and spoiled. She clearly harbored resentment and negative beliefs that were beyond any training I could offer her, so I had to let her go. This was a small sampling of her many negative beliefs that could destroy my practice.

Your ideal patient also affects your efforts to build community, your marketing, and your advertising. If you're good at speaking in front of an audience, doing so is a great way to establish yourself as an expert and connect with people who may have never heard of you. Any kind of speech or presentation requires a lot of time and preparation on your part and, remember, your time and energy are very valuable assets that you always need to protect. If your ideal patient was Sara, you would be most effective if you gave a speech to a local PTA. If your ideal patient was Cary, you would be most effective if you spoke to the charity board that she and her colleagues are involved in and support. Cary travels a lot and spends half of her time in airports, so if your ideal patient was Cary and you wanted to advertise to attract more patients like her, you would be successful if you advertised in magazines that appear in airports and on flights. However, if Sara was your ideal patient, you would be most successful if you advertised in parenting magazines and donated money to the local football team.

From the examples here, I hope you can see why it's important to identify your values, your boundaries, and what makes life fulfilling for you before identifying who your ideal patient is, why they are your ideal patient, and what values they honor. Knowing these truths is the foundation of every successful and profitable practice. These truths direct all your efforts and policies, office hours, the types of employees you hire, building community, marketing, and advertising. If, however, you want to do things the hard way, there is certainly nothing wrong with that, but you must have a very strong stomach to digest all the mistakes that you will make. As you will read in the chapters ahead, the universe has no problem testing your resilience.

Reflection Points

Before you start on this chapter's reflection, be sure to complete the ones from the previous chapter. Remember, you must know your values, boundaries, and what is fulfilling for you before you can describe your ideal patient.

1. Describe your ideal patient in detail. Explain why she is your ideal patient, i.e., how she matches your values.
2. Review your office hours to determine whether your current hours are aligned with the needs of your ideal patient as well as your own.
3. Write your financial policy based on the needs of your ideal patient, your values, and your boundaries.

CHAPTER 7:

Attracting New Patients and Nurturing Existing Ones

Every dentist I know is always looking for new patients—and for good reason. New patients are the lifeblood of any practice or business. Dentists are willing to spend massive amounts of money, or borrow massive amounts of money, to gain new patients because that means expansion and more production. However, what most dentists don't realize is that before spending advertising money to bring in new patients, it's important to assess a few key factors in your practice, such as current percentage of case acceptance or percentage of patients no-showing or cancelling confirmed appointments without giving proper notice. If your systems and policies are not set up correctly, you may gain new patients, but you may not retain those patients. The sum of those new patient visits may contribute to your goals, but they will not get you all the way there. They may even contribute to your problems more than your goals.

I usually ask my consulting and coaching clients what their new patient value is. Some clients don't know what that means, and some give me a very low number, which usually means something is not set up properly in their practice. Statistics show that gaining a new patient is seven times harder than keeping an existing one. Therefore, instead of putting all your efforts into getting new patients, it is worth spending some time reviewing how your existing patients are cared for first. You would be wasting your hard-earned dollars getting new patients if you have no active systems in place to care for, nurture, educate, and inspire existing patients to accept your treatment recommendations and share their positive experiences with others.

Unlike most coaches and consultants, I do not recommend directly asking your existing patients for referrals. This is a disaster. If you decide to do this, you might as well hang up a sign that states: "We're desperate and need more patients; please refer whomever you know to us." This is an awkward conversation to have with a patient, and there is never a good time to bring it up. Unless it comes up organically, I don't recommend spending time figuring out how and when to ask patients for referrals. Patients often feel they are not cared for or that it's not enough for them to show up and pay for treatment without being asked to either refer or write a review if you make a habit of asking. Instead, give patients plenty of reasons to talk and rave about you on their own.

Nurturing an existing patient doesn't involve doing anything extraordinary, but it does require consistency. Establishing trust—the foundation of any relationship—requires the ability to connect and to listen (visualize a heart with ears). Patients are not going to trust you just because you're a dentist or you have good online reviews or your name appears on the list of providers on their insurance plan. Reasons such as these may get them into your office, but they won't keep them there. They will rely on their own experience to determine whether they will stay or not and whether they will follow your recommendations or not. Being respected and valued are important in the doctor–patient relationship, but the core of establishing a relationship is your listening skills and your ability to connect with patients.

The reason a patient makes an appointment and then shows up is because they need something. They have a problem they believe you have the ability to solve. In the time that you interact with them, you will need to find out what the problem is that they believe you can solve and how they benefit from you solving this problem for them. It might seem very simple, but in many instances, it is not. There will be many obstacles in the way. You may ask, "If they have a dental problem and they need my help to solve it, why would there be any obstacles?" It seems logical to ask a question like this, but your patients are humans with complex lives. Based on logical thinking, which is a function of the left brain, the situation is simple: When a patient has a dental problem, they come to you and you solve their problem by treating them. They will pay you for this service, and you will both be happy. The reality is that when a patient has a dental problem, they will first choose a dentist to solve their problem for them. If that dentist is you, they will arrive at your office at their appointment time, they will complete all the new patient paperwork, they will tell you what is bothering them, you will do an exam and take the necessary x-rays, make treatment recommendations, discuss their options, as well as the consequences of not obtaining treatment, and tell them how much it costs. If they are in pain, they will agree to do what you recommend to stop the pain (most will accept the least expensive option or the one covered by their insurance), but if they are not in immediate pain, every resistance they have will come to the forefront and they will put the brakes on. They will make every excuse as to why now is not the best time for them to get the treatment done. They might even thank you for your recommendations, but they will not make an appointment to return. They will say they will call you after they talk to their spouse or significant other or after they get time off work or any number of different and creative excuses. The bottom line is that you will most likely never see this patient again.

Therefore, it's important that in your interactions with your patients, you discover not only what the problem is that brought them to you but also what they want (the benefit of solving their dental problems) in addition to the obstacles to you providing what they want. I hope you notice that I'm not using the word "need" and instead am using the word "want." You are trained to recommend what patients need; yet, patients will only act on what they want rather than what they need. For example, if, in your expert opinion, a patient needs healthy dentition, you can declare an endless number of reasons why that is important to their life. However, if the patient doesn't understand what benefit the dental work that you are proposing provides for them, they will only ask you to treat the pain in the one tooth that is bothering them and nothing else. They may believe that lack of pain means health, so why would they spend money and time tinkering around with the teeth that are not hurting? To keep them happy, you do an exam and take the necessary radiographs and treat the tooth that is bothering them. This patient will have received what she came for, but she may never return until something else bothers her and moves into her category of important. This new patient becomes an existing patient who spends less than $500 to treat her dentition per year because she has limited insurance coverage. She will be without pain but nowhere near the dental health that you know is possible for her. Even though you ask her to come in more frequently to get her teeth healthy, she doesn't see the necessity in that. Maybe she'll want some whitening at some point, but not anytime soon. This patient will never share her experience with anyone because it wasn't something she really cared about. She recalls her experience as this: "My tooth hurt, I found a dentist who fixed it, and I go back for a cleaning once a year. She wants me to come back more, but why fix something that's not broken?" If you have many patients just like her, the value of your new patients will only be $500. In this scenario, it makes sense that you constantly need new patients to increase or maintain your production numbers.

There are many reasons why a patient doesn't seek or want the oral health that you know is possible for them. One of the main reasons is an obstacle such as dental fear and anxiety. This was discussed in detail in my first book, *The Well-Referred Dentist, which was published on March 3, 2020*. Dental fear and anxiety may be caused by many things, such as past negative experiences or negative beliefs passed down through generations. Sometimes patients are not consciously aware of what is stopping them from obtaining treatment, which is why you're the one who has to identify these obstacles, and that begins by being curious and listening at levels II and III. [10]

---

10   Ibid.

Level I listening is when your attention and focus are mainly on yourself. As an example, you might be hungry and wondering what to eat for dinner while the patient is talking about herself and her dental problems. You may stop for a few minutes to buy in to the circumstances of the patient as she tells you that she has very limited insurance coverage and collude with her by offering the least expensive treatment, but your main focus is on yourself because it's close to closing time and you may want to get home before traffic starts and you assume that the patient will never agree to do anything other than fix the tooth that is bothering her due to her limited insurance coverage.

By increasing your curiosity and shifting your focus and attention to the patient, you can take your listening from level I to level II. At level II listening, your focus is completely on your patient, and at level III, your hard focus on the patient shifts into a soft gaze. Both your patient and her environment are the area of your focus. At level III listening, you will be able to access your intuition and hopefully have enough trust to share your intuitive insights with your patient. As the patient feels heard and understood, she will trust you more and will be able to consider your recommendations instead of feeling that she has to talk at uncanny speed in the hope that you will hear and understand her.

Remaining with the example above, at levels II and III listening, perhaps you'll find that one of the obstacles to treatment is her fear of not getting completely numb before treatment is started. Identifying that fear will enable you to reassure her that you will not start treatment unless she is completely numb and at any time during treatment, she can raise her hand if she's feeling anything and you will stop and give her more anesthetic. Knowing that this is one of her obstacles to treatment, after you take her into the operatory and anesthetize her, you may decide to give her a few more minutes to get numb. While she's getting numb, you'll ask her permission to take some intraoral photos of her teeth to show her how her other teeth are doing. Once you take her through a tour of her dentition with your intraoral camera, you can ask your front office team to copy the photos for her to take home while you treat the tooth that is hurting. Once you're done, you can take a few minutes to reinforce her positive experience by congratulating her for being so brave. You can let her know that a copy of the photos will be given to her and specify the next tooth to be treated because, by now, you may have discovered that she places high value on avoiding pain because she can't miss more days of work. If it's your policy to call all patients who receive anesthetic the evening of the appointment, you can tell her, "I'll be calling you later this evening to see how you're doing but you'll be numb for a while, so I don't want you to eat anything until I call you because I don't want you to unknowingly bite your tongue or lips and hurt yourself. Also, I'd like you to schedule your next appointment right now with [front-office receptionist] so we can make sure that you never have to miss work again due to having a toothache." By the time you call her that evening, her numbness is gone, she is out of pain, and even if you only talk to her for five seconds, you can end the call by telling her how well she did today and that you saw she made her appointment for next Thursday and you look forward to seeing her again.

After this appointment, she now has something to rave about. She will enthusiastically share with others the details of her wonderful experience and the kindness that you and everyone in your office showed her. She may be so inspired that she'll write a five-star online review before her next appointment and show up next week eager to treat the tooth that you recommended treatment for. She understands the benefit of treatment as never having to miss work again, which is of high value for her. All of this will occur without you asking her directly for a review or a referral.

The next step is to continue building the trust you started at this appointment. When this patient receives an appointment reminder call, make sure the person from your office makes this a friendly message by saying something unique and personal: "Hi, [patient's name], this is [receptionist's name] from Dr. Smith's office calling to let you know that Dr. Smith is looking forward to seeing you this Thursday at 5 p.m. If you have any questions, please call me at [xxx-xxx-xxxx]. You will get some automatic text reminders for your appointment, but I wanted to call you myself to see if you have any questions before your appointment. See you Thursday, [patient's name]." The exact words are not as important as letting the patient know that you (the doctor) know about their appointment and are looking forward to seeing them. The person calling has also left her name, so that's another person who knows she has an appointment and is welcoming her again. Usually, this call will be made forty-eight to seventy-two hours in advance of the appointment time so that if the patient has forgotten, they will be reminded and can make any necessary adjustments to their schedule. Depending on what kind of policy you have for no-shows or cancelled appointments, calling patients one day before the policy deadline gives them enough notice to cancel if they need to. After this call, they will usually receive automatic appointment reminders via text at twenty-four hours and four hours before the appointment time. These are all just suggestions. You will need to have a policy that reflects your process for patient appointments, and it will depend on your values, boundaries, and how you—as the doctor and the leader of the practice—feel most fulfilled. Your team members also need to be aware of and understand all the steps in this policy.

The greatest gift you can give to someone at their most vulnerable moment is the gift of empathy, compassion, and witnessing without judgment their thoughts and feelings. None of this can be possible without listening at levels II and III. When a patient feels heard and understood, they will be able to relax and trust your care. If at any point in patient care you are tested and wonder what the best way to proceed is, ask yourself if you are truly loving this patient exactly as they're showing up in that moment. What would love or compassion say? If, despite all that you do, a patient still has fears and anxieties, and if you are certified in The Fearless Way Method discussed in my first book, you can discuss and begin to identify and resolve the source of their fears and anxieties with their permission.

It is worth repeating that delivering the best dentistry for patients in the fastest amount of time with the utmost ease and comfort equates to both gaining a patient's satisfaction and profitability for the practice. It's every team member's job in the office to contribute to this outcome. Any patient's sole purpose for coming to our office is to get treatment. The entire time that a patient is present in our office, it has to be about them and not us. I recommend having a policy that captures this intention for everyone on your team, such as a policy that discourages having conversations that are irrelevant to the patient in front of them. As you practice your policy, you will become more aware of those times when you break it. For example, while treating a patient, you and your assistant realize you are engaged in a conversation that is irrelevant to the patient you're treating. You realize that doing so is giving the message that perhaps your attention is elsewhere and not on your patient. If you have an assistant who is given a five-minute task of cleaning the cement around the margins of a temporary crown and ends up spending thirty minutes on that task because she's giving every detail of her grandson's birthday party to the patient, that's also a problem. You will need to retrain this assistant on your patient care policy. When team members forget to focus on the patient instead of themselves, they need to be reminded of the purpose of their role in patient care.

Along with delivering excellent direct patient care, build the kind of community your patients will want to be a part of. Depending on what you like to be involved in, you may decide that a Facebook page is a community you will foster, or maybe it's a newsletter that you mail or email to patients. Whatever you do, it has to be something that your ideal patient has access to. If your ideal patient is a sixty-year-old professional executive, Facebook may not be their preferred method of engagement. If your ideal patient is a thirty-year-old stay-at-home mom with multiple children, they may love Facebook. This is another reason why it's important to identify who your ideal patient is; it will influence every decision and determine the direction you take in your business.

To reach a certain level of success, it is first wise to know who you're building a community for. Other examples of community besides the ones mentioned above might be throwing a monthly or quarterly dinner at a local restaurant. Offer to present a topic that is of interest to the attendees and take the time to answer their questions. You can let them bring one or two guests who are not patients of the practice. This is a great way of serving your patients while inviting referrals from those existing patients in a non-direct and generous way. The local restaurant will appreciate your business, and you can generate some buzz by writing about the event in your next newsletter or on your Facebook page. Activities like this may feel like a lot of work, but they pay dividends in the long run. The worst thing is when your existing patients don't know your name and they have to search for your card when someone asks them if they know a good dentist. You want them to not only know your name but to speak about you with so much love that the person inquiring feels like they found a treasure. Building a community fosters a connection with your existing patients that ensures they remember your name—fondly.

There are many other ways of fostering community as well. If you know how to do webinars, you can do one for your patients every quarter and have them invite their friends and family members to join. You can add some excitement by giving out small prizes for the three best questions. You can create healthy families or healthy friends campaigns where you host a gathering and create competition by offering prizes for the healthiest group in the previous quarter. Find different ways to brag about them as they get healthy together. These things show your existing patients that you can provide them with value even when they are not at your office. When life happens and someone they know needs a dentist, you want them to enthusiastically refer you. When they do, take time to be grateful. In fact, use these moments to give massive amounts of gratitude.

Make your patients feel better leaving your office than when they entered. Each patient, regardless of how well you know them, needs to feel that you see, respect, and value them. One of the best ways to accomplish this is to listen at levels II and

III, as we discussed earlier, and to express your gratitude for them. When people receive and acknowledge generosity from others, they're more likely to share that feeling through acts of kindness. Gratitude carries a high vibration of energy and has the ability to ground and center us. The way you give gratitude to your patients—or anyone—is important. Clearly describe what you're grateful for and how that person's actions helped or supported you. For example, if a patient always shows up five minutes early for her appointments and this is of high value for you, let her know how much you appreciate her promptness and how that helps and supports you. In the same way, let your patients know that you love knowing how you and your team have helped them and what that meant to them. Have cards in every operatory and in the patient waiting area, preferably not at the front desk, where patients can feel comfortable taking a card with a pre-stamped envelope that invites them to share their experience. It's best if the feedback given on these cards is sent to a location other than the office, such as a PO box, where you and only you will receive and read them.

The purpose of safeguarding your patients' feedback is to let them know they are safe and are always invited to share a negative experience with you without repercussions. You can't be everywhere at once, and you cannot oversee every intended or unintended slight. For example, one of your team members may unintentionally say something that upsets a patient. That patient doesn't know whether they're upset because of the information they received or because of the team member's tone. Whether this is a new patient or a long-term loyal patient should not matter. Depending on their communication style, this patient may choose to complain, but most patients will just leave your practice if they get upset. If they are sufficiently upset, they will leave the practice in addition to posting a negative online review, which won't be based on facts that you can investigate. If they were a loyal client, they are now pushed to a point where they don't care much about you and your practice and you'll notice small changes, such as not scheduling their next appointment, and they will wait until another upset occurs before becoming your worst enemy. Their reaction to the second upset will be cumulative and will seem out of proportion because you won't have all the facts from the first upsetting incident. So now this patient, who was always loyal, will turn into a disgruntled patient. Allowing circumstances to get out of control to the point where your loyal patients turn into your enemies is the number one worst mistake a business owner can make.

If through the implementation of this process, your patients feel safe and encouraged to share their experience, you may get a review that is positive. To show your gratitude consider sending them a small gift that you know will be special to them. If the circumstances feel right, let the patient know that you would love their review to be posted online. If the review is anything other than a five-star review, have a system in place to investigate what happened objectively and make corrections accordingly.

Online patient reviews that are negative can be damaging and upsetting. Having a system in place to investigate with clear action steps will enable you to view the situation from a more objective rather than reactive stance. This will allow you to stay in your power and not delve into a victim role, which is a very low energy state.

Many of my clients ask if they should join the chamber of commerce or business networking groups in their area. My answer is always the same: Visibility is important so that your ideal patients can find you. You don't want to be the best-kept secret in town. That would mean no one knows you exist. Once you are visible, you want to be able to make a connection with your potential ideal patients so that they can trust you and become your patients. The questions that I invite you to ask yourself are: What do you like to do and where do you like to be? Where will you be in your element and at your best? If you're an athlete and you love to play outdoor tennis in your free time, joining a tennis club is the best way for you to attract your ideal patients. Joining a networking group where you will be inside a building eating pasta at noon every week would not be right for you. This is why knowing your values and what you find fulfilling is so important. It really does affect every aspect of the steps you take for the success of your practice.

Another area to give attention to is making sure that you are operating at 100 percent efficiency. This includes having a front office team that is skilled at converting potential new patients who call your office into scheduled patients. Everyone on your team needs to be skilled at listening at levels II and III and knowing how to make a connection with a patient while focusing entirely on them. Your treatment plan acceptance rates should be 90 percent or higher, and every patient should have their recare appointment scheduled prior to leaving the office. Essentially, every aspect of your office operation and policies needs to be defined in writing, and your team members must be trained on each of those aspects.

Only once your practice is set up properly to provide the most value to your existing patients is it appropriate for you to spend money on advertising. Advertising is the most expensive way of gaining new patients. You would be wasting your resources if you spent money to gain new patients when you and/or your team are not 100 percent prepared to handle a new patient successfully when they come to you.

It is also worth mentioning here that insurance plays a significant role for some patients. Being a preferred provider for insurance plans is discussed in detail in Chapter 8, but the decision to accept or not accept PPO insurance plans requires a careful analysis of your practice. If you decide that your practice is ready to drop all insurance plans, a careful execution of this change needs to be planned so that it doesn't come as a surprise to any of your patients. Some of my clients decide to offer their patients a special savings plan as part of the change, which saves patients more money than their insurance plans and ensures patient loyalty. Just like any major change, it needs to be carried out carefully over time to minimize the loss of your ideal patients and, depending on the plan, make sure you do not break any state laws. Offering savings plans can also soften the blow when a new patient calls to make an appointment and finds out that you're not a PPO provider on their plan. Always plan for your long-term success, not just the short-term.

As I discussed, the reason I went through identifying your ideal patients in detail so early in the book is because once you know this important element, you will be able to not only love your ideal patients but also love the ones you have to let go. You cannot please *everyone*. If your mission is to help everyone successfully, you won't be able to help *anyone* successfully. There will be patients who won't be happy with the way you treat them or who will complain about your dentistry when there is nothing wrong with it. Some patients will find endless reasons for fault in you and your practice. Loving them means letting them go so they can find a dentist who better suits their needs. You also deserve to be respected, appreciated, and revered. You need to get paid in a timely manner so that you can continue running your business efficiently and profitably. Your needs and wants must be met. Over time, you will narrow down your ideal patient and start seeing your practice profit more without you being left with your essence extracted and only your stressed-out pulp remaining at the end of the day. As you read on, you will also become increasingly clear on what fulfills you!

In summary, the best way to bring in new patients is to treat the existing ones like gold. Loyal patients come through building trusting relationships, creating community, being visible, being accessible, and establishing yourself as an expert and a trustworthy source. Continually let your patients know about improvements you make or new procedures you add in a way that shows them the benefit to them and doesn't ask them for referrals. The only thing you want them to know when they complete a treatment with you is how much you're looking forward to seeing them again soon.

Reflection Points

1. Practice listening at levels I, II, and III with team members or your coach. Ask them to give you feedback on the impact that each listening level had on them.
2. While listening at levels II and III, identify the problem that a patient has and write it down in their words along with the impact of this problem on their life. How will the patient benefit when this problem is solved?
3. Practice presenting treatment plans only after the problem, the impact of the problem, and the benefit of solving the problem in the patient's own words is clear for you and the patient is confident that you have

heard them. Track the success of your treatment plan acceptance.

4. Write a patient care policy that clarifies the steps each member of your team will take to deliver excellent dentistry in the least amount of time with the utmost ease and comfort for every patient.

5. Have feedback cards available in each operatory and patient waiting area (somewhere other than the front desk) with a stamped envelope addressed to a location other than your office.

CHAPTER 8:

Accepting or Dropping Insurance

Insurance is one of those subjects that I believe every dentist thinks about every day. There are a great many factors worth considering when you are deciding what—if any—insurance your practice will accept, and you must decide which options are best for you and your practice. In this chapter, I offer my experiences and some practices for evaluating and deciding what will work for you, but, ultimately, the decisions about insurance are yours alone.

Now, I can't thoroughly discuss HMOs because I never accepted them myself. I will, however, share a couple of stories about my two—and only—experiences with a dental HMO office that contributed to my decision not to accept them in my practice.

Between the time that I resigned from my associate job and purchased a practice, I worked in different offices as a temp. One of the offices required me to do their hygiene patients that particular day I was assigned. I noticed that every patient who came in that day had severe gingivitis or periodontal disease. However, I didn't find any notations in their chart that they had been diagnosed or recommended treatment. They all seemed to be on a six-month hygiene recare cycle. So, while cleaning their teeth, I proceeded to let them know about the condition of their gums and recommended deep cleanings to treat their gum disease. After the fourth or fifth patient, I was interrupted and asked to see the owner dentist in his private office. As I entered his private office, he closed the door behind me and sheepishly said, "You're doing a great job recommending treatment to these patients and there's nothing wrong with what you're recommending, but you have to understand that under their HMO plan, deep cleanings are not a procedure that we get reimbursed for and so if we perform it, we have to do it for free. We don't recommend it for that reason."

Hearing those words for the first time was like having daggers thrown at me and what I knew to be right and true. He was practicing supervised neglect, and he was asking me to do the same. As I briefly mentioned in an earlier chapter, one aspect of supervised neglect is when a doctor, knowing that there is disease present requiring treatment, chooses to not inform the patient and does not recommend treatment. My first response was deep shock and disappointment. I told him that I could either leave right then and there or I could stay and finish the day. If he wanted me to stay, I would do so under the condition that I would continue informing patients of the true condition of their gums, but I would also add that treatment was not covered by their insurance plan and they needed to speak to the front office to find out the fee for treatment. He agreed, and I completed the day under those terms and never returned.

Naïvely, I didn't know whether all offices were like that or if it was just this one. On another day during my time as a temp, an offer came to work in an HMO practice. I hesitantly accepted, against my better judgment, and showed up to the practice ready to start my day. I was handed a ten-page document that I was required to sign without being given any time to read it. I asked the gentleman who handed me the document to give me a quick summary. As he was summarizing the document, one aspect stood out for me so much that I hardly heard anything else. I don't remember the exact wording, but it was a paragraph that said should a patient sue me for malpractice, I accept full responsibility for any grievance and will not hold the corporation responsible for anything. He then proceeded to ask for my malpractice insurance and license and when everything was signed and copied, he said I could start.

My first patient was an eighteen-year-old young man who needed a crown cemented on his upper front tooth. After trying the crown on his poorly prepared tooth, I quickly realized that this crown was never going to fit properly on this tooth. I proceeded to explain to the patient that I would recement his temporary crown back on his tooth, and I recommended that he return for an exam so a new treatment plan could be discussed and we could proceed from there. I had five minutes available to cement this crown before I moved into another room to treat the next patient, so I didn't feel there was adequate time to recement the temporary crown, do an exam, and discuss my recommendations with the patient. I could feel the heavy stare of the office manager on my back as I said goodbye to the patient. She pulled on my jacket before I crossed the threshold of that operatory to tell me that I didn't have the right to tell the patient that his crown didn't fit. She said, "You should have just said that the dentist who had prepared the tooth will be cementing it and that he should reschedule to be seen by that dentist."

She was not interested in hearing why the crown did not fit properly. I was bewildered about why, if all crowns had to be cemented by the same dentist who prepared the tooth, this patient was put on my schedule. She said that "the dentist had called in sick." Soon I realized that this HMO office did not care about how well the dentistry was done. As long as something was put on the patient's tooth resembling dental work in as short of an amount of time as possible, they were satisfied. I told that manager that as long as I was the treating dentist, I would perform dentistry the way I knew was right. I told her that she was welcome to do my job, but since she was not a dentist with a license to practice, she couldn't. So, at least for that day, she had me and only me to do the work. I was not about to be bulldozed by someone who was not a dentist and yet gave herself permission to be disrespectful in her communication and question my expertise. I spent the rest of the day handling patients who had been triple-booked. At one point, I had one patient in one operatory needing a root canal, another one needing four wisdom teeth extracted, and in the third operatory, I had an eight-year-old child with six cavities to treat. It was 6 p.m. and we had to close at 7 p.m., which meant I had one hour to treat all three patients.

At the end of the day, I went over to that office manager to say goodbye. She said, "I was surprised and impressed that you came back after lunch."

I replied, "I came back because I committed to being here today, but I will not be back tomorrow or ever again." I asked one of the full-time dentists there how he managed to sleep at night knowing the kind of dentistry he was performing. He said, "Patients have a choice to get their treatment done in a private office and pay for that treatment. When they come here and don't pay anything out of pocket, they know they're getting a band-aid, and I'm here to provide that band-aid." He said this as he proceeded to start a three-unit bridge preparation for a young man within the thirty-minute time period allotted.

I left that office feeling like I had compromised myself and my values, and it was not a good feeling. I thought to myself that if I ever had to practice dentistry and accept HMO insurance plans, that would be the day I would walk away from dentistry and change careers. I had friends who built their offices successfully by accepting HMO plans and learning how to profit by upselling their patients. The gist of HMO plans is that they require a dentist to charge a patient a very low fee for some procedures and do others for free. Often, UCR fees are reduced by 90 percent. In return, the plan will send the office patients who are assigned to that office. In addition, if a patient never sees the dentist for any treatment, the insurance plan will pay the dentist a minimal per capita amount per patient, just for being on the list of patients for that office. So, it's in the best interest of the dentist not to see patients for cleanings and routine exams because they are free under most HMO plans. Instead, the dentist would sell patients on procedures that were not covered by their insurance plan because, in those cases, they could charge patients an additional fee.

Outside of those two experiences, I have no knowledge of HMO plans and their potential for profitability. What I do know is they were not for me. I will not discuss whether they are useful or right or wrong other than sharing the fact that accepting HMO plans is one way some dentists choose to build their practice. The decision of whether or not to accept HMO plans depends on your values, your boundaries, and what you find fulfilling in your work life. I can assure you that you cannot be an office that accepts all of the different insurance options: HMO plans, PPO plans, and UCR plans. Your office can only be set up to operate one way. You can only successfully accept a few top PPO plans, UCR plans and patients without insurance if you're set up to deliver excellent dentistry, and HMO plans do not pay for excellent dentistry.

To use an analogy, consider shopping at Costco versus Whole Foods. Costco sells everything in bulk and has cheap prices. Whole Foods is known for selling organic foods. They don't sell anything in bulk, and they're not known for being cheap. Small business owners go to Costco to shop for their yearly paper supplies, spend $300, and purchase in bulk. They would not go to Whole Foods to make such a purchase. However, they will go to Whole Foods to purchase organic cookies for a client they're having a meeting with who they know only eats organic products. They will gladly spend $300 to entertain this client for one afternoon.

The decision to be a preferred provider for PPO insurance plans has to be made carefully after evaluating your practice. If you are considering purchasing a practice, find out if this practice already accepts any PPO plans. If they do, find out which ones and become a preferred provider for each and every plan in that practice before you purchase it. You don't want to make any changes for at least the first year after you purchase this practice, especially to insurance. If you do make changes, expect to lose 50 percent of the patients immediately. People don't like change. When their dentist changes, that's enough of a big change. They may tolerate one big change, but two big changes will result in them putting on the brakes and they will find another dentist faster than you can blink. In your purchase agreement, remember that you have (hopefully) paid for goodwill. Don't let that go to waste.

The way that a patient views their dental insurance plan is very different from how you view it. For most patients, their insurance plan is a security blanket, even though we know it's not much of one. Most patients don't know what is offered to them and may think their dental insurance is the same as their medical insurance. Since you understand the language of their dental insurance plan, it's best that they hear an explanation of their benefits from you. If you don't, someone else will and may set false expectations for them. Once patients know that they can go to their dentist for information, they will come to realize that they can trust their dentist. Once that trust exists in one area (such as insurance), it will spill to other areas as well. By consistently receiving true and accurate information from you, they will learn that they can trust your recommendations—and the treatment that you perform too.

Most dental insurances have a $1,500 yearly maximum. Patients think of that as cash that is handed to them every year. Some patients hesitate to use that and hold on to their insurance in case an emergency comes up. By informing them properly, you can help them understand that they can use that money to make sure that emergencies don't happen. Help them understand that the money is not handed to them in bulk. As they get treatment done, a percentage of that amount (based on the category of procedure) is paid to their dentist. For example, if they get a prophylaxis and polish done, this procedure belongs to the preventive category. Their insurance may pay 100 percent of preventive category procedures after the yearly deductible has been met. The deductible, which is usually around $50, has to be paid by the patient first before their insurance covers the rest of the fee. Each dental insurance plan has many variations, so it's best to obtain a fax of the patient's benefits at the yearly start of their plan.

Before you prepare a financial arrangement for treatment that is to be rendered, an update needs to be done on the phone with the insurance plan. There are computer software programs that do that for you, but I've never found them to be accurate because your software only has knowledge about treatment that you have performed on the patient. If your patient had a root canal done at another office and the claim is outstanding when you're about to do a crown on their tooth a day later, you will not know what percentage of their benefits will be paid to the endodontist unless you call the insurance carrier and ask. Even then, that is not a guaranteed amount being paid to the endodontist's office. Sometimes the patient's employer changes insurance plans in the middle of the year and the patient doesn't know or fails to give you that information. So, you bill the old insurance and, after waiting thirty days for payment, you might receive a letter that states the insurance was terminated before the date of service so there is no payment due to your office. Now you need to call the patient and ask them what insurance they have and start the process all over again, send a new claim in, and wait another thirty days to get paid. Anyone facing this situation will get aggravated with the patient and the circumstance. Suffice it to say a lot of preparation needs to go into understanding a patient's insurance benefits so that payment delays such as this don't happen.

There are many factors worth considering when you're evaluating whether being a preferred provider on a plan is worth your time and effort. First, determine how much money you need to collect each month to be able to pay your bills, your employees, and yourself. This will be your minimum collection target number (MCTN). To find your actual collection target number (ACTN), add your collection per month for the last six months and divide the total by six. If your ACTN is lower than your MCTN, do not drop any insurance plans that you're a PPO provider for. Instead, request a fee increase every year. A fee negotiation has to be done in writing. Before submitting your request, carefully read the policies of each insurance plan. They may allow fee increases every year or every two years. Submit twenty to twenty-five procedure codes that you most commonly perform and ask for increases on those codes. Let them know how much lower the fees are for their plans as compared to your UCR fees. Express how well you care for your patients and inform them of the excellent quality of dentistry you deliver. Every insurance plan wants high-quality dental offices on their list of providers because if patients complain to their employer about their dentist, it will reflect negatively on the insurance plan and when it comes time for renewal of the plan, the employer will not renew their contract if there have been a lot of complaints.

If you do the exercise above and find that in the last six months, your ACTN has been above your MCTN, especially if it has been higher consecutively for three months in a row, do some digging to find out what you did in those months where your collection exceeded your MCTN. It's important to keep notes weekly or monthly so you can track your successes and failures. When you track your progress, you can better understand what actions led to higher collections and do more of those actions. You can also see what actions or incidents led to not doing well so you can correct them before they become a consistent problem. This is also how you make your policies clearer and better. I have asked you to look at your collection numbers first because that is money you tangibly have in the bank to pay your bills, your employees, and yourself. Once you have determined your ACTN, you can figure out how much you need to produce in order to meet your ACTN each month. To figure out your actual production target number (APTN), look at your production (using UCR fees) for those same six months, add each month's production and divide the total by six. For example, you may find that each month in the last six months your actual production (APTN) was twice your collection (ACTN). In other words, each month you collected half of what you produced due to insurance write-offs. This is only accurate if all the write-offs were related to insurance and none was unrelated, such as senior citizen discounts. This will provide you with a fairly accurate ratio of production to collection. In the example above the ratio of APTN to ACTN is 2:1. Now you can apply this ratio to figure out your minimum production and collection numbers (MPTN and MCTN). For example, if your MCTN is $30,000, you will know that in order to collect this amount you need to produce $60,000 (in UCR fees) each month.

If you find that being a preferred provider for a specific insurance plan does not work for you, the decision to drop that plan needs to be made carefully and will depend on the following factors:

1. What percentage of the new patients who call your office state that the reason they chose your office is because they saw your name on the list of dentists on their insurance plan? To be certain about the accuracy

of the answers, your receptionist needs to be skillful at recording and obtaining correct answers without being too interrogative and driving a new patient away.

2. Some insurance plans are so popular that even if a new patient calls your office because they heard about you through your advertising, they still want to be sure you accept their insurance plan before they decide to come in. Therefore, the popularity of the insurance plan should play a factor in your decision.

3. Does the insurance plan allow for fee increase negotiations every year or every two years on your twenty-five most commonly used procedure codes? If so, how much increase can you expect? How long does the negotiation for fee increase take?

4. Does the plan do automatic fee increases every year or every two years without caring about your input? If so, what is the percentage increase?

5. How quickly does the plan pay a claim?

6. How often does the plan delay payment to your office because they need additional information, even though you have offered all the pertinent information?

7. How often does the insurance company state that they have not received your claim even though you know you sent it?

8. There are some insurance plans that exclude payment for certain procedures. For example, at one point, United Concordia did not pay for root planings (deep cleanings) in the absence of bone loss evident on radiographs. Not only that, but as a preferred provider, you were not allowed to collect any money from the patient if you performed root planings. Something like

this from an insurance company would force you into supervised neglect, which is below the standard of care. This hopefully would be against your values and render your decision firm, clear, and non-negotiable to refuse to be a preferred provider with that plan.

9. Evaluate the quality of the patients who are on an insurance plan. If most of these patients fall outside your ideal patient profile, that plan may not be right for you.

10. Be sure that if a plan does not pay for a procedure code that they allow you to charge your UCR and not a certain percentage of your UCR or anything other than your full UCR fee. It is against the law for an insurance plan to dictate fees for a procedure code that they don't cover, i.e., when an insurance plan does not cover a procedure code, they cannot dictate the fee for that procedure in any manner.

11. If an insurance plan makes a mistake and pays in excess of what they are supposed to pay, as long as they are not a self-funded plan, when they write to you asking for a refund to correct their mistake, you are not obligated to comply with their request. For more information and to obtain a sample reply letter, you can reach out to your state's division of the American Dental Association (ADA). These requests often cause great angst for a dental office, because now you have to contact a patient—who may or may not be an active patient at this point—and ask them to pay you more money because of their insurance plan's mistake. Even if you do everything correctly and supply a copy of the insurance plan's letter to the patient and explain that it was the insurance plan's mistake, it will leave the patient with some resentment

toward your practice. Insurance companies need to bear the responsibility of their mistakes without involving the dental office. If an insurance plan does this even once, I would recommend assessing your tolerance of these mistakes against the value you receive from being a preferred provider. You also need to consider your values and boundaries and evaluate whether this crosses any lines for you before making a decision. It is, after all, your practice.

The above eleven factors provide you with a solid foundation for making the right decision about accepting certain PPO insurance plans, but there is usually a lot more to consider that will require a full evaluation by your consultant and/or coach. If anyone tells you to drop all insurance plans without getting to know you, your values, your boundaries, and what you find fulfilling in your work life, along with conducting a thorough evaluation of your practice, I would highly recommend that you send them on their way.

If you decide to accept some PPO insurance plans, know that educating your patients at every step of the financial arrangement process is key to a successful relationship. In your financial arrangements, always let patients know what your UCR fee is and that if for any reason there are problems with the insurance plan, it is their responsibility to pay you the UCR fee rather than the PPO fee. Financial arrangements will be discussed in more detail in Chapter 10.

For now, look at the amount that the insurance plan offers a patient every year as a gift for that patient. Use this to teach them the importance of taking care of their teeth, but also let them know that to reach and maintain healthy dentition will require them to invest more than the maximum per year that their insurance plan allows. That amount is simply considered a good starting point for health. If they hear this truth repeatedly from you and your team, they will get used to it and it won't be a shock to them when they have to invest beyond the $1,500 or so provided by their plan.

There will, of course, always be patients who make it clear that once they have used up their maximum benefits, they will want to postpone any pending treatment to the following year. Remember that your job is to educate them in a way that is understandable to them using a lot of examples and analogies, but, ultimately, they are responsible for their decisions and their health. As their doctor, you can guide them and make recommendations, but you can't take their choices away from them. Patients need to know that they are the ones who are ultimately responsible for their health—not you. Similarly, you are the one who is responsible for setting policies for your practice. Those policies need to reflect your values and your boundaries in a way that is fulfilling for you. Otherwise, you will open the door to resentment and, before you know it, you may get burned out or depressed and end up not wanting to continue in the profession that you love and have invested so much in.

I wish I had a crystal ball to see whether being a PPO provider for every PPO plan that exists is the right choice for you. But we both know that such a crystal ball doesn't exist. And I'll say it again. If anyone tells you to drop all your insurance plans, please run the other direction. I have seen colleagues do this and lose their practice in a very short amount of time. If you purchase a practice where the seller is part of any PPOs, make sure you have signed up for all the PPO plans that the seller was a preferred provider for before you purchase the practice. I mention this again because when I purchased my practice, the seller didn't tell me that he was part of many PPO plans. As a young dentist, I didn't know that this would be a significant factor in patient retention. Even if I did, I wouldn't have known how to verify the truth of what he told me. I did lose 50 percent of that practice's patients within twelve months. Even though I realized that most of his patients had PPO plans and joined all of them within three months of purchase, in most cases, it was already too late.

If after doing a thorough evaluation you still find that your left brain, your intellect, and the numbers are not enough to make a decision, pay attention to your body. Do you feel expansion or contraction when you consider being on PPO plans and writing off half your treatment fees? What about when you consider not accepting any PPOs and possibly losing your practice because you don't have enough production to keep the doors open? If there is more contraction from the latter scenario versus the former, that could help put things in perspective for you. Remember, you can always change course when you're more established and profitable, but even then, making a change in insurance requires careful evaluation and preparation to ensure success.

Reflection Points

1. Make a list of the PPO insurance plans that you accept, if any.
2. Read the policies of each plan and summarize the main points.
3. Select twenty to twenty-five procedure codes that are most often used in your practice.

4. Add the dates for fee increase requests to your calendar so that requests are sent out promptly.

5. If you have decided to be a PPO provider for an insurance plan, evaluate their value in your practice every quarter by using the information in this chapter as a starting point. For a detailed review, meet with your consultant and/or coach.

CHAPTER 9:

Production—Creation and Manifestation

One of the most important first steps for any dental appointment is truly listening at levels II and III and asking questions to get to know your patient and what they value. Everyone is more than eager to speak about what they love and find fulfilling in their life. By honoring a patient's values, you can build connection and trust with them. Treatment recommendation should come last to maximize the chances of that patient accepting your treatment recommendation and increasing production.

I once had a patient named Tom who was also my IT person. I relied on him heavily to keep my computer servers functioning optimally at all times. One day, he said he wanted to get his teeth cleaned. I scheduled him for a same-day appointment. When he came to work on our computers, I always paid for his services that day. I truly appreciated how he was always readily available to fix anything IT-related, so I wanted to return the favor by being available to clean his teeth. We had formed a trusting relationship … or so I believed. Tom was self-employed and didn't have dental insurance. He was married with six children under the age of fifteen. During that first appointment, his teeth were cleaned above the gumline, but the exam revealed that he had stage II periodontal disease. I explained the condition of his gums in detail and spent time recommending treatment, reviewing his options in detail, and letting him know what would happen if he didn't follow my recommendations. Loss of his teeth and the infection in his mouth adversely affecting his general health were possibilities I discussed with him that day. I did everything by the book as I was taught to do. I even gave him a 30 percent discount, which was the highest discount I could offer. This discount meant that if he accepted the treatment, his payment would just cover my overhead.

Months passed without Tom getting any further treatment. One time, he began the recommended treatment but didn't complete it. I thought maybe he didn't want to be treated by me, so I offered to send his records and x-rays to another dentist or periodontist of his choice. He always said no and deferred his consideration to another day by saying, "Soon, Doc, soon." I finally had to dismiss him from my practice for non-compliance. Months later, he came to my office one day to do some IT work, and he looked as if he had lost weight and had been working out with weights. As usual, I asked him whether he had obtained treatment for his gum disease. Instead of answering my question, he shared that he had been going to the gym five days a week consistently and taking care of his body. Physically, he seemed to have developed very well-defined muscles and appeared to be in an extremely good mood.

He said, smiling, "Don't worry; I'm more fit and healthy than I have ever been in my whole life. Just look at me, Doc!" He had not asked for his x-rays to be transferred to another dentist after I had dismissed him from my practice for non-compliance. He was clearly choosing to not receive treatment from anyone. Since he was at my office that day to fix my IT problems and was no longer an active patient in my practice, I didn't inquire any further.

The following day, I called his cell to ask him about a problem I had encountered from the previous day's IT work, but hours went by without a reply from him. This was unusual; he always replied promptly. Later that afternoon, I called his office and his receptionist answered the phone announcing that Tom had passed away at the gym the day before while he was working out, leaving his wife and six children behind. She was devastated and said everyone else was too. They were all wondering why he had a heart attack when he was healthy and in such good shape. Unfortunately, even though he looked as if he was in the best health, he wasn't healthy.

I was devastated too. I kept replaying the number of times I felt like a broken record, pleading with Tom to get the much-needed dental treatment I had repeatedly recommended but he had refused. I had done everything by the book, and I kept wondering why I had not succeeded in getting him to accept my recommended treatment.

Research has shown that oral health affects the health of the rest of the body, including the heart. I had shared this repeatedly with Tom, but he failed to do anything about it. He, as well as many other patients, believed in: "If it doesn't hurt, why fix it?" I couldn't help but wonder how else I could have painted a picture for him that he could understand. How could I have done

108 | The Foundation of Profitable Dentistry

things differently so he would have accepted the recommended treatment for his gum disease? I wondered how many other patients had died at least partially because of untreated gum disease.

Other than forcing him into treatment, which is not possible, I had no solution. And that just wasn't enough for me. This incident was one example among many others that propelled me to start searching for better ways of getting through to my patients, which eventually led to discovering and implementing The Fearless Way Method. In addition to this method, I learned that my treatment plan acceptance rates increased when I got to know my patients' values and how dental treatment would benefit their lives.

In Tom's case, he may have valued his six children more than he valued his own life, so the benefit of dental treatment in his case would have been being around long enough to see his children become adults with their own lives. Letting Tom know about the condition of his gums and recommending treatment so he could become healthy before knowing what he valued most in his life was unsuccessful. Instead (assuming this is what he valued most), saying the following may have worked better, "Tom, I know how much you love your kids and I know you want to be around for a long time to care for them and then to see your grandchildren. I wish I could be sure that you can do that with the existing condition of your gums, but I don't see that possibility. Gum disease is tricky because it doesn't hurt. It's like the computer virus that hides in your computers until one day, without notice, all your computers crash. The only thing you might see is a little bit of blood when you brush your teeth or feel your teeth becoming loose, but other than that, you won't know you have this disease until the infection in your mouth affects other parts of your body, especially your heart. The same way that the computer virus can kill your computers, this disease can kill you without notice."

If this kind of conversation is handled effectively using language that a patient can understand, it won't be long before the patient agrees to the treatment. Because their most important value is presented to them, every other value takes a back seat. In Tom's case, values such as saving money would no longer drive his decision because being alive and providing for his six children was the most important value for him.

If a patient is not ready to hear all your treatment recommendations, telling them their entire treatment plan up front will be completely ineffective. Doing so before you have even gained a patient's trust will damage any chance of ever developing that trust. As dentists, we've been taught to inform our patients about the condition of their teeth and recommend treatment, as well as discuss all their options and the consequences of not obtaining treatment. We all agree that the ultimate aim is to get the patient to optimal health. However, our patients are not robots. The path to optimal health requires the inclusion of the human element of trust and connection. Getting to know your patients and their values is the most effective way to get them healthy.

While getting to know your patients, another tool that proves very useful is having the knowledge to discover and identify where energy has impeded flow in your patient's physical body. In *The Well-Referred Dentist*, I wrote in detail about how negative thoughts create negative emotions. If these negative emotions are not resolved, the continuous disruption of energy flow can eventually cause disease in the affected organs of the physical body.[11]

To illustrate this, let's look at another patient. Cindy presents as a healthy, fifty-six-year-old, single female who takes pride in taking care of her health. She shares that she has been to the Scripps Institute, which she considers the mecca of the best physicians in the world. She's been given the good news that her health couldn't be better. She has been told that she is as healthy as a thirty-year-old and she wants her teeth to reflect this health as well, so she requests that veneers be placed on her teeth.

Cindy had been my patient for over fifteen years. I knew her to be level-headed and very responsible. She always showed up for her appointments and paid for her treatment, even though she had no insurance, but I had noticed that lately she was complaining about fees. I had a gut instinct that she was shopping around for a less expensive office. This was just a hunch. I had no tangible proof of this whatsoever. She did grind her teeth, and I had recommended she wear an occlusal guard at night, which she had been wearing faithfully. I had no reason to mistrust her about having received the perfect health score from the Scripps Institute. Per her request, I provided her with an estimate for twenty veneers (ten teeth each for her upper and lower teeth) along with a new custom-made occlusal guard to replace the existing one after the cementation of the veneers.

She called back the day after I gave her the estimate and asked for an itemized report of the recommended treatment and the procedure codes for each item. She was so nice about it that even though it was against my policy to provide patients

11 Ibid.

with procedure codes and itemized fees, I agreed to provide her with everything she had requested. The feelings that I originally had about something being off had now escalated. I brushed the feelings away again and despite my gut guiding me in a different direction, I reviewed her cosmetic expectations and had her sign a document giving me permission to start the treatment. She paid for the veneers, and two weeks later they were cemented after gaining her approval of their appearance. I proceeded to make the impressions for the occlusal guard and sent the models to the lab to fabricate it. Even though I had asked the lab to put a rush on them, there was still a wait time, so I gave Cindy explicit instructions not to eat anything hard along with all the other instructions necessary for her to prevent chipping her newly made veneers. I even went as far as making her a soft guard, which is not ideal, but it was meant to prevent fractures of the veneers as a temporary solution until the occlusal guard was ready. Her occlusal guard was delivered within forty-eight hours, and she left my office very pleased. So was I ... until she called my office three days later with a chipped veneer.

In summary, the area of the chipped veneer indicated that Cindy had not worn her occlusal guard at the time that her tooth chipped. She was very unhappy, and so was I. I had taken every precaution and made sure the occlusion was perfect, so how could this happen? The veneer had to be redone, and the work that was done for fabrication of the new occlusal guard had to be redone and postponed until after this veneer was remade and cemented. This was one of the reasons that Cindy decided to find another dentist who "understood her body better."

Intuition is that soft voice that whispers and informs us about situations we have no tangible proof of. When trusted, it can lead us to the truth much quicker than we could otherwise hope for. Some mistakenly believe that intuitive sight is a gift or skill bestowed on a lucky few. The truth is that we all have intuition, but whether we follow that intuition or not is based on our level of trust in that subtle and small voice. You must have the self-esteem and level of maturity to understand your intuition and have the level of personal power to witness it. Our intuition, like any other skill, can be developed and fine-tuned with practice.

Knowing about and being trained to identify energy flow problems is immensely useful in treating human beings who are impacted by their emotions. It turned out that Cindy had a drinking problem. Although she managed it, sometimes she dealt with negative feelings by drinking heavily and passing out. Although her intentions were to always wear her occlusal guard, when she passed out, she was not in control of her good intentions.

Her energy flow was impeded around her throat (fifth chakra), heart (fourth chakra), feet, and below her hip (first chakra). *Chakra* is a Sanskrit term meaning "wheel of light." In *Vibrational Medicine*, Richard Gerber (2001) describes chakras as being multi-dimensional and specialized energy centers within the subtle bodies which "take in and process energy of higher vibrational nature so that it may be properly assimilated and used to transform the physical body."[12]

In Cindy's case, there had been changes at her work and she had been asked to leave after twenty years of working for the company. She had no say in it. Because of this, it was

---

12   Gerber, Richard. *Vibrational Medicine: The #1 Handbook of Subtle-Energy Therapies*. Rochester, VT: Bear & Co., 2001.

no surprise that she had impeded energy flow to the chakras mentioned above. She felt that she had lost her voice (throat chakra), she was worried about her future (first chakra and feet chakras), and she was incredibly sad to have lost her job (heart chakra). Although she had decided to improve her smile by getting porcelain veneers, she had realized that her problems were not resolved by the new smile. Her recent drinking episode ended with her passing out and chipping her veneer. Her pride and financial situation prevented her from sharing this with me at first, and the guilt of lying about it resulted in her changing dentists. She did not share the truth with me until a year after she had switched to a new dentist.

If I had trusted my intuition and had known how to identify energy flow problems, I could have helped Cindy understand that perhaps this was not the best time for her to start all this dental work. It is not our job as dentists to know about intuition and energy flow problems, but these are tools to help us know and connect to our patients, who are human beings with emotional, mental, and spiritual aspects as well as physical. It's worth remembering that we are treating the whole person and never just the teeth alone, so the more tools we have, the better we can serve our patients and the less stress we create for ourselves.

If a dentist believes in and supports a holistic model of healthcare, she is in a position to help her patients accept and recognize the value of seeing the connection between their emotional stresses and the health of their bodies. Patients like Cindy or Tom often don't want or are not in a place to accept the responsibility and do the work required to get healthy. Since the holistic model of healthcare requires the patient to be an integral part of the healing process, without the patient's participation, it is not possible to heal them. Cindy carried her stress in her jaw and her temporomandibular joints. Conventional dentistry offers a properly fabricated occlusal guard to protect the teeth and the restorations on these teeth, but the real reason for why a patient engages in such activity can only be found at the source of their stress.

Although I teach about the chakras and their functions in detail when I work with my clients, my wish here is to provide only an introduction, much like planting a seed with the intention of piquing your interest to learn about this worthy subject in more detail. I must add that once you are properly trained in this work and you are clear that you want to include it in your practice, you will attract patients who want to do this work as well.

You may find—or you may have already discovered—that the dentistry you were taught to do and would like to do is very different than the dentistry desired by patients who refuse to take responsibility for their health and have handed the reins to their dental insurance plan. You might be frustrated that your days are limited to practicing within the confines of a patient's insurance coverage and that you are struggling to educate your patients so they can understand that their health deserves so much more than what their insurance plan allows in terms of yearly coverage. This is yet another reason why identifying your ideal patient is a key factor in attracting the right patients to your practice. If you want to treat everyone, you will bring in a huge array of patients, including those who are not ready to do the work. But when you get really clear on your intention of wanting to do this energy work, you will attract patients who are either ready or seeking and willing to learn more.

As an introduction to this work, let's talk a little bit about chakras. There are seven main chakras in the physical body, and they operate similar to a relay team. The energy of one affects the others, which is similar to how we, as physical, emotional, energetic, and spiritual beings, affect each other as well as all creation.

The first (root) chakra, known in Sanskrit as *muladhara*, is located at the base of the spine, more specifically, at the coccyx. The first chakra is akin to matter in its density and is involved in survival instincts and grounding. It brings the individual solidity, stability, focus, and form. The energy of this chakra affects the immune system, physical body support, base of the spine, legs, bones, feet, and the rectum. The immune system is the protective army of the body and is directly related to the survival aspect of this chakra. The immune cells are mostly created in the flat bones, the largest of which is the coxal bone (the hip). The energy content of this chakra is comprised of tribal/family power, which refers to group identity, force, willpower, and belief patterns. One example of tribal power can be seen in families where becoming a doctor, lawyer, or engineer are the only acceptable and respected careers, so adolescents pursue these paths without ever questioning their decision. Another example would be a patient who comes to your office for dental treatment but doesn't follow all your recommendations because her family believes that if it's not broken, you don't fix it.

The second chakra, known as *svadhishtana*, is located in the lower abdomen between the first chakra and the navel area. It is akin to movement, involved with the desire for pleasure and merging with another. It allows the individual to experience difference, change, and movement, to embrace polarities, and to discover passions of difference, choice, emotion, and desire. This chakra relates to the flow of power between the self in relation to others. It provides energy to the reproductive organs, large and small intestine, kidney/bladder, and lower lumbar vertebrae. The physical dysfunctions include severe premenstrual cramps, endometriosis, ovarian cysts, fibroids, constipation, diarrhea, gas, and chronic lower back pain. This chakra represents choices. As dentists and business owners, you are forever reminded to make your choices wisely because each choice you make is a creative act of spiritual power for which you are held responsible (Myss).[13] The second chakra challenges us to learn what motivates us to make the choices we do. The choices we make are influenced by either our faith or our fears, and the outcome reflects the same.

Anodea Judith (1987) says, "Where the first chakra seeks to hold on and create structure, the second chakra's purpose is to let go and create flow. Flow allows one thing to connect energetically with another (109)."[14] One of the challenges dentists experience with their patients is creating an environment that is safe enough for patients to let go and allow flow; yet, at the same time, be completely grounded in their body.

The third chakra, *manipura*, is located at the solar plexus above the navel. This chakra represents energy with the purpose of overcoming inertia and bringing about transformation. It has to do with personal power in relation to the external world. The third chakra's function also has to do with our vitality and dreams. In the body, it relates to metabolism. In psychology, it relates to enthusiasm followed by the ignition of power and

---

13   Myss, Carolyn. *Anatomy of the Spirit: The Seven Stages of Power and Healing.* New York: Harmony Books, 1996.
14   Judith, Anodea. *Wheels of Life: A Users Guide to the Chakra System.* St. Paul, MN: Llewellyn Publications, 1987.

will. In behavioral terms, it brings about activity. It is the fire of our will that propels the movement of energy from the first to the seventh chakra. It is our will that propels us into action, allowing us transformation. Energetically, this chakra correlates to the stomach, spleen, pancreas, adrenals, upper intestines, gallbladder, liver, and the lower thoracic spine. The dysfunctions and illnesses that originate in the third chakra are activated by issues related to low self-esteem, low self-confidence, low self-respect, low self-responsibility, fear of rejection, oversensitivity to criticism, power struggles and associated anger, excessive generalized fear, and difficulty making decisions, in addition to the internalized issues and trauma that caused them. The illnesses that may ensue as a result are chronic or acute indigestion, gastric ulcers, pancreatitis, diabetes, anorexia, bulimia, liver dysfunction, hepatitis, adrenal dysfunction, mid-back pain, and lethargy or fatigue in the morning upon waking.

Earlier, I mentioned that self-esteem is an important aspect of intuition. Self-esteem develops our inner personal power so that we can tap into our unlimited potential to transform our lives, strengthen our spirit, and heal from past emotional traumas and existing illnesses. In her book *Anatomy of the Spirit*, Caroline Myss says, "If your spirit is strong enough to withdraw from the authority of a group belief, it is potentially strong enough to change your life." (175).[15] The independence of the third chakra is related directly to our intuition, giving us the confidence to take risks and follow our gut hunches. For us to understand our intuitive guidance, we must have the self-esteem to recognize that intuitive guidance isn't a clear voice telling us exactly what to do, but is a feeling, perhaps akin to discomfort or confusion,

---

15   Ibid.

directing us to make difficult choices that will break us out of stagnation and misery (Myss).[16] If someone doesn't believe in the intuitive information, the door doesn't open for clearer and more accurate information to arise. If you suffer from low self-esteem and are afraid of failing, it will be hard to act on your intuitive impulses. Intuition is only effective if you have the personal power and courage to follow through on the guidance received. As Myss states, "Guidance requires action, but it does not guarantee safety." (181).[17] In addition, working with our intuition doesn't mean that we get to bypass our fears. Our intuition is more aligned with our spirit, which pushes us to grow bigger, and that oftentimes means facing our fears. True intuition is not aligned with our ego, which wants us to always stay safe.

The fourth chakra, known as *anahata*, is located at the center of the chest, and it represents the central point of the chakra system. It is akin to air and is considered the least dense of the physical elements represented by the first to third chakras. Air is about spaciousness, which is primarily achieved through letting go. This chakra provides energy to the physical body through the heart and the circulatory system, ribs, breasts, thymus gland, lungs, shoulders, arms, hands, and diaphragm. Anodea Judith (1987) explains, "This is our spiritual center, our core, the place that unites forces from above and below, within and without." (192).[18] The fourth chakra is the center of compassion. It teaches us how to behave from a place of love and compassion and helps us realize that love is the most powerful energy we possess. It mostly aptly teaches us about

---

16 Ibid.
17 Ibid.
18 Ibid.

caring for ourselves and others and how to maintain a healthy balance between your emotional needs and those of others. The dysfunctions and illnesses that originate in the fourth chakra are activated by issues related to an inability to feel or express love for oneself or others, feelings of loss and grief, anger, hatred, resentment, self-centeredness, and inability to forgive. The illnesses that may ensue as a result are myocardial infarction (heart attack), congestive heart failure, asthma, lung cancer, pneumonia, upper back/shoulder problems, and breast cancer. This entire book is written with the fourth chakra's influence in mind to help you see yourself, your patients, and everything about your practice through the eyes of love—and not just any love but the fourth chakra kind of balanced love.

Two necessary attributes of the fourth chakra that go hand in hand are self-love and forgiveness. Forgiveness does not mean that what someone did to hurt us is okay. As Caroline Myss states, "Self-love means caring for ourselves enough to forgive people in our past so that the wounds can no longer damage us—for our wounds do not hurt the people who hurt us, they hurt only us (204).[19] By releasing our attachment to our wounds, we give ourselves permission to move from the first three chakras' childlike relationship with the Divine (or Universe or whatever you believe in) to the fourth chakra's ability to act out of love and compassion. To think like a wounded child will keep us trapped in the cycle of loving conditionally, along with being stuck with an immense fear of loss. Regardless of how your heart is broken, you always have the choice of figuring out what to do with the pain. By choosing to forgive, you can take away

---

19 Ibid.

the power of fear, thus releasing the authority of the physical world over yourself.

Facing daily challenges and change is common in the life of a doctor who is also a business owner. To keep yourself in flow with life, engage often in genuine forgiveness (both for yourself and others), practice being in appreciation and gratitude (even when seemingly minimal), live in the present moment, and know that change is a necessary aspect of life as important as breathing, the purpose for which is allowing us expansion and advancement of the spirit. Most importantly, at the end of each day, let go of the day with loving-kindness in any form that best serves you. I try to imagine being in nature and changing my path slightly to invite rest and reflection … breathing deep one breath at a time, slowing down with every in and out, coming into the present, one slow breath at a time. Try this and, if you find that it works for you, take it one step further. With each in breath, set the intention to take in love from the universe through the top of your head and allow it to fill every cell of your being. With each out breath, allow love from your heart to flow through and extend out into the universe to flow to others who might need it too. Even though this might be a challenging practice, it is a worthwhile one, as love is the key to finding happiness, which essentially lies inside you.

Although there is not enough space to go into the details of these practices in this book, there are lots of good resources out there, and I also go through these practices in detail with all of my clients.

In *Wheels of Life*, Anodea Judith (1987) states "Communication is the process of transmitting and receiving information through symbols." (236).[20] The fifth or throat chakra, also known as visshuddha in Sanskrit, is the center of communication, creative expression, and the power of will (how will is manifested in physical form). Located at the throat, this chakra produces communication through sound, vibration, self-expression, and creativity. The throat chakra translates these symbols of communication into information (Judith, 1987).[21] An open and flowing fifth chakra allows someone to communicate their feelings with confidence and know that they are being heard. They are able to express their personal truth and are willing to recognize and utilize their creativity without fear of criticism. The opposite is true with an obstructed fifth chakra. This chakra is connected energetically to the physical body in the areas of throat/pharynx, thyroid, trachea, esophagus, parathyroid, hypothalamus, neck/cervical vertebrae, mouth, jaw, teeth, and gums. Blockages in the fifth chakra are related to disease in the above areas, such as thyroid problems, chronic neck pain, or periodontal disease.

Most of the patients who have problems with their dentition have varying levels of blockage in their throat chakras. However, since each chakra is connected to the next, an energy disruption in one affects all the others to one degree or another. Identifying and clearing the source of the negative emotion that caused the disruption of energy flow helps to make sure that once a patient's dentition has been restored to health through dental treatment, they will *remain* healthy. If the source of the energy disruption is not known, delivering excellent dentistry alone will not keep the patient healthy in the long-term.

---

20 Ibid.
21 Ibid.

Effective communication in any setting is important, but in a dental office it is vital as many of the patients requiring dental treatment may have blockages in their fifth chakras. Energy flow disruptions in the fifth chakra affect a dental practice's production and collection numbers more than energy flow disruptions in any other chakra. Communication that is effective (positive, kind, and helpful) strengthens your connection with your patients and serves as a source of stress resilience, well-being, and peace for them.

I previously discussed the importance of pre-appointment reminders from the office staff and post-appointment calls from the doctor. They are worth mentioning again and cannot be emphasized enough. These calls create a structure for the patients that has a beginning, a middle, and an end. Everyone loves structure and a sense of completion. The doctor's call communicates empathy and compassion that continues beyond the appointment itself. Patients often feel a great deal of gratitude when they hear from their dentist after their treatment. Even though the conversation often does not extend beyond one or two minutes, the message that it sends to the patient is one of genuine care. Since gratitude fosters gratitude, it is often in these moments when genuine compassion and care extended by the dentist inspire the patient to become a loyal patient and refer others without the dentist ever asking.

The sixth or third-eye chakra, also known as *ajna* in Sanskrit, is located in the center of the forehead. It is the center of insight, clairvoyance, and intuition. When this chakra is open and flowing, the individual is able to see the truth in any situation, is open to the ideas of others, and is able to be present. They are also able to maintain a balance between intuition and analytical thought. In other words, when this chakra is healthy, the individual is able to experience a deep connection to their inner voice and is able to receive and accept inner guidance. They will also be able to understand the larger truth of a situation versus the smaller truth of the ego's needs, wants, or desires. A healthy sixth chakra also helps a person engage in adult consciousness and witness aspects of self, which are the parts of self that are wise and neutral. However, when blocked, the individual will engage in dogmatic/judgmental thinking, will rely excessively on logic and analytical thought, will fail to see the truth in any situation, will doubt and not trust themself, leading to a feeling of inadequacy, and will be unable to learn from experience. This chakra is energetically connected to the physical body in the nervous system, brain, pineal gland, hypothalamus, pituitary gland, spinal cord, peripheral nerves, eyes, ears, nose, touch, and taste receptors.

This chakra is also associated with the law of detachment. It is through being detached and healing the traumas you have endured that you can reach a sense of peace. In *Anatomy of the Spirit*, Caroline Myss explains that detachment does not mean lack of caring. Instead, it means quieting one's fear-driven voices so that, with practice, you will be able to attain an inner posture of detachment. In doing so, you can experience or have a sense of self so complete that external influences will fail to have any authority over your consciousness. Myss states, "Such clarity of mind and self is the essence of wisdom, one of the Divine powers of the sixth chakra." (239).[22] This is useful for both the dentist and the patient. Earlier in Chapter 5, I wrote that the Universe will throw whatever you have not resolved at you until you learn the lesson you need to learn. What we

---

22   Ibid.

have not resolved will keep us attached to our negative feelings and, in turn, will attract other low-energy behaviors, such as Don's (the patient who was initially happy with his veneers but then came in 2 weeks later first thing in the morning ready to attack) behavior toward me. If I had not been so attached to my low self-confidence as a young and inexperienced doctor running a business, I would not have been affected as much as I was by Don's negative behavior. Tania's story below is another example of how sixth chakra imbalances can affect a patient in your practice.

Tania was a new patient in my practice. During her initial appointment, she mentioned that she was very afraid of dental treatment and had avoided seeing a dentist for five years. During this visit, I was not able to successfully perform a thorough exam and take the necessary radiographs that I needed in order to diagnose her dentition properly. Besides verbalizing that she was afraid, she also exhibited all the signs of an extremely fearful dental patient. Her distress score from a scale of one to ten (with ten being the highest level of distress) was ten. Her chief complaint was that the previous dentist she went to did not speak fluent English. Therefore, he did not understand her when she wanted to communicate that she was not sufficiently numb while he was working on her. Instead, when she moved her head away from him, he got very upset with her and complained to her mother that she was not a cooperative patient. She felt her communication fell on deaf ears, which resulted in unfair criticism. As a result, she suffered a great deal of pain. The feeling that she was not able to get her voice heard had become a pattern in her life and now was being repeated in her relationship with her husband.

Tania was in her mid-twenties and had impeded energy flow in her fifth and sixth chakras. A brief view of her dentition showed that her gums were inflamed, her teeth had visible cavities, and most were worn down due to bruxism. Her health history revealed that her thyroid was sluggish. She expressed that her immediate wish, more than needing to be healthy, was to communicate with her husband without fear of criticism regarding what she needed in order for their relationship to be successful—that was her biggest value over dental health. She had tried to speak to him many times previously, but she again felt that her communication fell on deaf ears. She cared about him deeply and this was clearly a difficult situation, as she did not want to hurt him or appear to be a demanding person placing ultimatums on their relationship.

After obtaining permission from her, during a different visit that did not include any dental treatment, we restored the flow of energy to her sixth chakra. (The process for doing this is something I go into in more detail with my clients. It is simply too much to include in this brief introduction to energy work.) Once energy flow to her sixth chakra was restored, she was able to see the truth in her situation and separate the matter from illusion. She was able to detach from the result (possibly involving a divorce) knowing that regardless of what happened, she and her husband would be fine. By restoring flow of energy to her fifth chakra, she was able to honor her choice to have a conversation and accept any possible consequences of that choice. The sixth chakra governs the law of cause and effect, so by grounding her physical and energetic body (in addition to her sixth chakra), she was able to quiet her conflicting voices and choose instead the wise voice of her inner essence guiding her to honor her truth, goals, and desires. By properly using the healthy fifth chakra's power of choice and communication, as well as the fourth chakra's openness with love, she was able to choose her words to her husband in a way that exhibited her truth with love (with no intention to hurt or dishonor herself, her husband, or the relationship) and trust that the universe would take care of the details. By the end of our session, she appeared to be at peace and said she had not felt this relieved for years. To my surprise, she asked to schedule her next dental appointment. She was then able to keep all her dental visits and completed her dental treatment with ease and comfort. She remained a loyal patient for many years and referred many friends and family to my practice.

It took sixty minutes to assess which chakras had impeded energy flow for Tania. Through applying energy medicine methods of grounding and meditation, the energy flow to all her chakras were restored. During this time, she was heard and, for the first time in her life, she felt safe in the presence of a dentist. Using The Fearless Way Method would have been equally successful but, intuitively, I felt that a shorter method might be just as effective for her and the successful results showed that trusting my intuition was the correct way to proceed. This patient was able to proceed through multiple dental appointments and became healthy. Had I not recommended this sixty-minute session for her, she would have walked out of my office after her first visit and never returned for another one until she was in pain. The trajectory that she was on would have resulted in the loss of many teeth before she reached her sixties, and she would have suffered silently by avoiding the dentist's office like many other patients do.

As the seat of cosmic consciousness or enlightenment, the crown or seventh chakra, also known as *dahaswara* in Sanskrit, is located at the top of the head. In the same way that a king's crown signifies order in his kingdom, the seventh chakra signifies the ruling principle of life. It connects us to divine intelligence and the source of all manifestation. It is through this chakra that we are able to know, reach understanding, and find meaning. Meaning is a pattern that connects things, bringing us closer to unity and linking the individual to the universal (Judith, 1987).[23]

It is through the seventh chakra that the human life force energy originating from the greater universe enters the physical body and pours endlessly into the human energy system. Caroline Myss explains in *Anatomy of the Spirit* that this force feeds the body, mind, and spirit as it distributes itself throughout the physical body and the lower six chakras, connecting the entire physical body to the seventh chakra. The energy of the seventh chakra influences the nervous system (some brain function), the skeletal system, the muscular system, and the skin.

The seventh chakra also allows us to access an infinite amount of information through our experiences and allows the awareness of the mind to play it out like a movie. As we watch this movie of thoughts, our mind puts together the information gained from experience, gives it meaning, and eventually constructs our belief system. This belief system then becomes the master template from which we construct our reality (Judith, 1987).[24] It is from within that we can access limitless storage capacity, and it is through meditation that we can explore this inner world. To fulfill our highest purpose, it is essential that we learn to navigate both the outer and the inner world of

---

23   Ibid.
24   Ibid.

thoughts, feelings, memories, desires, and imagination, as well as look deeply at the belief systems that we have created from our experiences that were traumatic on any level. Until we do that, we are running movies that are more in alignment with ego protection than our soul's purpose.

The mind always tries to find meaning behind most activities. We have often heard people ask, "Why did this happen to me? What is the meaning behind all this?" The search for meaning allows a person to integrate an experience. Once we understand the meaning behind a situation, we are given a basic operating system from which we are able to cope, operate, and flow with the situation. It connects us to a sense of higher order from which we can integrate the rest of our experience into wholeness (Judith, 1987). [25]

Meditation is the best way to develop the seventh chakra. It is through this practice that consciousness realizes itself. Meditation helps us to realize that the mind is not the master and instead is merely a servant. Pure consciousness and unity with the universe are the ultimate masters, and meditation gives us this experience. Anodea Judith (1987) explains, "Each of the chakras is a manifestation of consciousness at different layers of reality, with earth being the most dense, and the seventh chakra, as its opposite, the pure unmanifest consciousness, known in yoga philosophy as *purusha.*" *(323).*[26] Consciousness is described as a force that brings unity, order, and organization. It is the ordering principle that is inherent in all things, from the structure of a molecule to that of a building or a city. There are many different types of meditation available for practice,

25   Ibid.
26   Ibid.

but one aspect that all meditation practices have in common is that through focusing the mind on one thing, they quiet or declutter the mind of previous thoughts and activities. With regular meditation, a person can achieve a state of deep rest while increasing their attention and awareness.

The seventh chakra contains the energy that brings about devotion, inspirational and prophetic thoughts, transcendent ideas, and mystical connections (Myss).[27] The mental and emotional dysfunctions that originate from an unbalanced seventh chakra include the inability to trust life or feel in control of life (absence of meaning and purpose), diminished sense of self (loss of self-identity), and an unwillingness to recognize and connect with the spiritual element of life. These are the essential elements in experiencing the "dark night of the soul." Caroline Myss says that illness is often a catalyst to spiritual transformation that can come from the "dark night."[28]

As dentists and business owners, you know that a perfect day in a dental practice rarely happens. There are always forces and circumstances beyond our control that test us to our core. When I moved my practice to a different location, the tasks that had to be accomplished were endless. The more I did, the more there was to do. In a moment of frustration, one day I posted on my personal Facebook page, "How do I get rid of my to-do list?" At the time, I had no idea how much power my words carried. Soon after posting that question, my servers crashed and brought my entire practice to a halt. In addition, my sweet dog Pumpkin, who I loved beyond words, was diagnosed with cancer. Sometimes everything must turn upside down to get our

27 Ibid
28 Ibid.

attention. My servers crashing certainly got my attention, but Pumpkin's diagnosis brought me to my knees.

It was at this time that my migraines started. The servers were fixed and Pumpkin had successful surgery, but my migraines persisted every day for endless months. I had experienced painful headaches before, but migraines were a different ball game. My head felt like a pressure cooker without a release valve, and there were many moments when I had my fingers on my phone worried that I would need to call 9-1-1.

When all the medical exams and tests came back negative, I realized that the stress in my life was most likely the cause. There was no medicine that I could tolerate that would alleviate the migraines. I even tried acupuncture with no success. Finally, my father, who never believed in meditation, recommended it as a last resort. Having nothing to lose, I enrolled in a class to learn Transcendental Meditation (TM). I was very skeptical since I had tried mindfulness meditation before without success, which is why I chose transcendental meditation this time. The basic difference between these two types of meditation is that mindfulness aims to train the mind to continually return its attention to an awareness of the present moment, usually via the breath. On the other hand, through repetition of a specific mantra, TM effortlessly liberates the mind to transcend thought altogether. The state of being that becomes available through TM is more profound than the present moment. It is a state that is more restful than sleep. Because of the connection between the mind and the body, when the mind is at rest, the body follows accordingly, letting go of its deepest stresses. Within weeks of meditating every day, my migraines became less frequent and less severe in intensity. This allowed me the space I needed to identify what triggered the migraines besides stress. I realized that I had a chemical sensitivity to products such as perfume and cologne in addition to sensitivities to foods containing certain ingredients. With diligence and a few lifestyle adjustments, I was able to dodge the bullet of being flattened by migraines within a few years.

Sharing this personal experience about my health is not intended to be a promotion or advertisement for TM but is an example of how being open to other modalities that are not mainstream or conventional literally saved my life when prescription pills and other medical treatments brought intolerable side effects. The migraines stopped me in my tracks long enough for me to surrender and learn the deeper lesson of letting go of my obsessive need to control and to hold on so tightly for fear that everything will fall apart. Meditation was my release valve. By allowing me to connect to myself and to the universe, it provided me trust in a higher order. Somehow, I felt more protected than I ever had before. Having survived the "dark night of the soul" in a surprising way expanded my consciousness. As a result, I became a better person and could provide service to my patients in ways that I couldn't have without this experience.

You might be thinking, "Wait, wasn't this chapter about production?" And I wrote about everything other than production. That wasn't an accident. I know that each one of you as a licensed dentist is more than qualified to diagnose the dentition of human beings and make correct recommendations, along with discussing all the options available and the consequences of not following your recommendations. I see no reason to repeat what you have already been trained to do. Your patients are human beings with an array of past negative experiences, negative beliefs that may or may not have been handed down from generation to generation, and a physical body that is so enmeshed with their emotions and thoughts that it's hard to discern one from the other. They have lives full of complex challenges and emotional wounds that even they may not be fully cognizant of. So, to say that your production is dependent on how many teeth you treat would be a huge misunderstanding of who you are as a healer.

Healing is not linear, and it's not only about fixing teeth and gums. You most likely can take one quick look at your patient's dentition and x-rays and know exactly what treatment they need in order to have healthy dentition. However, to truly get them healthy requires you to listen to and connect with them. Instead of leading with what you know, which is the dentistry, listen to and get to know the human being in front of you. Allow them your attention and love so they can trust you. When you know them well enough, you will be able to speak to them in a way that they can comprehend and that reveals a benefit to them in terms of what they value. Then, and only then, should you recommend the dentistry that they need and want. This and The Fearless Way Method constitute the foundation for getting a firm "yes" to all your treatment recommendations.

Getting to know your patients, connecting with them, establishing trust, knowing how to speak to their values, and identifying how they will benefit if they follow your recommendations in a way that they can understand does not require lengthy amounts of time. It only requires curiosity, levels II and III listening skills, the willingness to witness and genuinely care for their entire being, not just their teeth, and seeing them through the eyes of love despite how they show up on any given day. If you can do this each time they come to your office, you will gain a loyal patient—a loyal human being—who will refer others to you and rave about you more genuinely and effectively than any advertisement or promotion ever could.

Reflection Points

1. Do timed exercise drills where you and another team member talk to one another about a subject and see how quickly you are able to decipher what the other person values most in their life.
2. Describe one time when you ignored your intuitive insight and one time when you followed it. What were the results of each situation?
3. Review a random health history and, based on the physical diseases noted, identify which chakras have impeded energy flow.

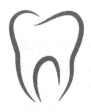

CHAPTER 10:

Collection—Timely Payment for Your Expertise

The most important step in establishing and maintaining trust with patients is centered around preparing, obtaining agreement for, and honoring written signed financial arrangements. Your collection policy is one of the most important policies that you'll ever write, and this too is dependent on your values and boundaries. The purpose of writing down your collection policy is so that everyone on your team is on board and follows the policy ... including you. Once you write your collection policy, reflect on this question: "What would have to happen for me not to honor my collection policy?" Answering this will allow you to tighten your policy and clearly establish your boundaries.

Many of my clients are torn when they hear sad stories about why patients cannot afford treatment or need more time to pay their bill. After all, you want to help those who need your help. You are kind and generous and exceptionally altruistic. These are phenomenal qualities that everyone who knows you cherishes. However, you have bills, salaries, and yourself to pay. You're running a business that needs to be profitable to survive. Before you write your policies, knowing your numbers is extremely essential because they show you the reality of what you need to do to stay in business. If it's important to you to do charitable donations or to offer free dentistry to a certain segment of the population, be clear about the purpose of doing this and whether you can afford it. Don't randomly decide to give discounts each time a patient announces that they can't afford your fees. What I have often found is that when patients realize that dental treatment is in alignment with their values and benefits them, they will find a way to come up with the money to pay you.

For this chapter to make sense, keep in mind this premise: Each time you bill a patient, always bill your Usual, Customary, and Reasonable (UCR) fees. Once you receive the insurance plan's payment, enter that payment in the patient's account, then enter the write-off at that time. As I wrote earlier, MCTN is your minimum collection target number. This number is the minimum amount of money you need to collect each month to be able to pay the practice's bills and the salaries of your team members and yourself. This is a bare-minimum, non-negotiable amount of money that has to be in your bank account each month. The next number that you need to know is the average percentage of UCR fee write-offs you do each month due to your agreements with the PPO plans that you accept. To calculate your average write-off percentage (AWOP) simply follow the steps on the next page:

1. Choose the most common PPO insurance plans in your practice.
2. Choose twenty-five procedure codes that your office bills most often.
3. For each PPO plan, add all the fees associated with these common procedure codes and divide the total by twenty-five. This will give you an average PPO fee for each plan. Then add each plan's average PPO fee together and divide this total by the number of PPO plans in your office to get an average PPO fee for all the plans that you are participating with.
4. Do the same for your UCR plan with the same twenty-five codes. This will give you an average UCR fee. For example, let's say that your average UCR fee is $200 and your average PPO fee is $60: 60x100/200 tells you that your average PPO fee is 30 percent of your UCR fee. Therefore, on average, you write off 70 percent of your UCR fees when you see PPO patients (100 percent - 30 percent = 70 percent). Although this is not an exact number, it will give you a general idea. This also means that you need to see 3.33 PPO patients to make the same amount of money that you would make seeing one UCR patient (100 percent x 1UCR patient / 30 percent = 3.3 PPO patients). If 100 percent of your practice is comprised of various PPO plans and you never offer any services that are charged at UCR fees, then you would know that to make your MCTN, you have to produce approximately 3.33 times more than your MCTN. If your MCTN is $30,000 each month, then your MPTN (always in UCR fees) needs to be 3.33 times more. This equals $99,900 if 100 percent of your office is PPO. If

50 percent of your office is PPO and 50 percent is UCR, then the amount of MPTN will change accordingly.

If your office accepts several PPO plans in addition to seeing UCR patients, it is best to work closely with a consultant to obtain a more accurate AWOP. Once you're clear on these numbers and have reflected on what you value, you can write your collection policy. Make sure your team understands it and knows their part in honoring this policy. Your collection policy and each team member's job description associated with your collection policy become part of the agreement that you have with your team members. For example, if your policy states that patients are to be presented with a financial arrangement and their co-payment collected prior to start of treatment, your team needs to know who presents the financial arrangement, who gets the patient's agreement and signature, and who collects the co-payment. If this needs to be done prior to start of treatment, is this done at the front office or in a consult room (if you have one) or is it done in the operatory after the patient is seated? Is this done by a staff member or is it done by the doctor? Every dentist has their own preference. My recommendation is for you to do everything in your practice at least once and become good at it so that you can train a team member if the current person responsible for this task calls in sick, quits, or is let go.

When fees need to be discussed, you must be able to look your patients in the eye and state the cost of treatment in a firm, yet loving, way. If you choose to delegate this to someone else in your practice, be sure to present a few financial arrangements yourself at least a few times a week as practice. If you can do this consistently and naturally with ease, you're in your power and your patients will pay you or request a financial arrangement.

Either way, it needs to be a clear decision made by you and them according to your financial policy. If your discussion of the treatment recommendations is done properly (as described in Chapter 9), this part will be a formality.

The financial arrangement (FA) is nothing other than another piece of the agreement that needs to be made and followed to ensure trust between you and your patients. The following areas need to be covered in order for the patient's expectations to be set accordingly. To receive a sample worksheet on how to calculate a patient's co-payment amount and a sample financial arrangement to be signed by patients, please go to www. drbitasaleh.com to request a copy of both.

Once patients pay their co-payment, they don't appreciate receiving a bill a month later from you to pay your office more money because their insurance didn't cover as much as you thought they would. Therefore, it's very important to do your due diligence before presenting the FA to them. Insurance plans often provide a detailed account of a patient's benefits via fax. It usually takes thirty minutes for someone on your team or you to decipher this information in a way that is quickly accessible. Some dental software programs are very savvy at using this information, as well as the treatment you plan to complete, to calculate the amount that a patient will need to pay as co-payment. Regardless of whether you have a dental software that can do this or not, it is always best for you and your team to know how to do this by hand if need be. This can be done with an insurance benefits form that includes most of the procedure categories you perform and the percentages that the patient's insurance covers, as well as certain other details like yearly maximums and deductibles. Once you have this information in a quickly accessible format, the worksheet to calculate a patient's co-payment will only take a few minutes to figure out. Then the patient's financial arrangement form needs to be prepared, presented, and signed by the patient. It might take you, depending on how extensive the treatment plan is, anywhere from five to twenty minutes to complete this process by hand. Using Excel or a program in your dental software will make this calculation a lot faster. Considering how much time it takes to collect from a patient three months after you have completed their treatment (sometimes up to five hours in addition to harboring negative feelings or potentially losing a patient), it is worth taking those initial twenty minutes to set up agreements that lead to trust and timely payment.

Correctly assessing a patient's co-payment is dependent on two factors: One is knowing every detail of their insurance plan benefits and limitations and the other is knowing the descriptions of dental procedure codes and the circumstances in which they can be used. You don't want to allow a patient's insurance limitations to ever dictate the direction of treatment, but it is beneficial to both you and your patient to maximize proper reimbursement. For example, an existing patient who recently had their recare done at your office and was billed for a periodic exam as part of the services they received calls you a few months later needing urgent treatment for a chipped front tooth. The patient's chief complaint is that the jagged area is hurting their tongue. After examining the tooth and taking an x-ray, you let the patient know that the chip is small enough that you can smooth it out for now to prevent it from agitating her tongue and she can return next week for follow-up. The patient agrees and you smooth out the tooth and polish it. If you bill their insurance for an emergency exam, which is a correct use of this code, your claim will be denied. Why? Because even though their plan covers two exams per calendar year, this policy only covers exams when they are six months apart. However, if you did not perform any other procedures on the patient that day, you can use code D9110, which is a palliative procedure code that can be billed in ten-minute increments. By including an explanation, you will most likely get reimbursed. Therefore, you maximized your patient's insurance and took care of them in a time of uncertainty and discomfort without allowing insurance limitations to dictate the direction of patient care. If your office had told this patient at the time of her initial call that she would need to pay for the exam out of pocket because her insurance would not pay, she may have never come in that day, choosing to suffer until the next week when you had time to see her. Based on her level of discomfort, she may have even found another dentist to see her—one who would have not asked her to pay for the exam because they would have known how to correctly bill insurance for reimbursement—and you would have lost a perfectly good patient.

Your UCR fees reflect reasonable fees based on your expertise, experience, and the time it takes to complete a procedure. If a reasonable fee for a simple extraction is $200 and it takes you ten minutes to numb and extract a tooth, you should not discount your fee because you're faster than another dentist who takes thirty minutes to do the same procedure. Similarly for other procedures, charge a fee that reflects your expertise. If it takes you less time to complete a procedure than it takes another dentist, this would be considered a benefit for the patient. There is no valid reason to charge less because your expertise and experience allows you to deliver excellent dentistry faster than another dentist can. In the same token, many dentists do not value their expertise when it comes to diagnosis and therefore do not charge for it appropriately. For example, taking an x-ray may incur a $25 fee, but the diagnosis requiring your expertise incurs another fee, which often is included in their exam. However, if you're taking a full-mouth series of x-rays for a new patient, doing a full examination of their teeth and supporting structures, spending thirty minutes or more of your time preparing a treatment plan, and spending an additional forty minutes presenting the treatment plan, you need to charge for the x-rays, the exam, and the treatment plan preparation and presentation separately. There are procedure codes for each of these; yet, dentists often do not charge for the latter. If a practice has mostly UCR patients, the dentist may decide to include the fee of preparing and presenting even complex treatment plans in their exam fee or in their treatment fees. But if you accept PPOs where 70 percent of your fees are written off, it doesn't make sense not to charge for your expertise, time, and experience, regardless of whether those fees are covered by a patient's insurance plan, as long as you inform the patient ahead of time that it's not covered. If you're willing to give away your time and expertise without charging for it, you're sending the message that you don't value your time and expertise. If you don't value yourself, why should patients or your team members value you?

Once again, reflect on who your ideal patient is based on your values. Keep reflecting as you gain experience and expertise until all your decisions and policies fulfill you as a person, as a dentist, as a business owner, and as a leader. If you discover that you might have limiting beliefs in the area of money and profitability, bring it up to your coach and work diligently to clear those beliefs that no longer serve you. An example of a limiting belief is: "All wealthy business owners are greedy."

Consequently, you will unconsciously prevent yourself from becoming profitable so that you are not placed in the same greedy category that other profitable people are placed in.

At the heart of every human being lies the desire to reasonably reciprocate for what we receive. In addition, it's human nature to not appreciate something as much when it is given to us for free versus having paid for it ourselves. Patients usually want to pay properly for receiving something that they value. Most don't want to overpay, but they also don't want to not pay or underpay. They want proper exchange. If you don't charge them for presenting their treatment plan or other services, those services will not appear as valuable and will not be taken seriously. I once had a patient who needed extensive dentistry tell me that she couldn't afford her dental work because she wanted to do a kitchen remodel. She ended up not having enough teeth to properly enjoy tasting the food she was able to make after the remodel of her kitchen. I had another patient tell me that he couldn't afford to take time off from racing cars to come get his periodontal treatment done. He died of a heart attack within a year of his visit while he was racing a car. In my first year out of school, when I was practicing as an associate in a dental practice (as I mentioned in Chapter 2), I had to remove all the teeth of a thirty-five-year-old lady who had suffered from severe periodontal disease and deliver immediate dentures to her in the same appointment. At that point in my career, I had never seen someone age so fast in front of my eyes due to losing their teeth. It was an experience that I never forgot.

These along with other examples of patients who suffered the consequences of not following through with recommended treatment helped me understand that, as dentists, we have the responsibility of finding ways to help patients understand the value of treatment and the consequences of not completing the recommended treatment. This understanding gave me the courage to look many patients needing dental treatment straight in the eye and recommend, as well as charge a reasonable fee for, my expertise and the time spent helping them understand why it was important to get treatment. I did this because I wanted them to see the value of being healthy and take responsibility for that. If they paid a dentist to get healthy, they were more likely to value and maintain that health. I set my boundary in that if I did my job of presenting value and did everything else that was in my power to do and the patient, having been given a reasonable length of time to comply, still did not initiate treatment, they would be asked to leave my practice. Non-compliance was one of the reasons that I dismissed patients, and that was my boundary. Our experiences often bring to light what we value and I never again wanted to witness the disappointment and sadness on a patient's face who had been an active patient in a dental practice for quite some time and tell them they had to make the decision to extract all their teeth because none of them could be saved.

When you charge a patient for your time and knowledge, you are sharing the truth of what you know because of the expertise that you have worked so hard to gain. You are charging for results, not five or ten minutes of your time. The units of time are irrelevant to the outcome of saving someone from losing their teeth—and potentially their life. Most of the time, one of the most effective ways of allowing a patient to see the value of what you see is to charge them a fee that gets them to pay attention to their health.

After the write-offs that you are contracted to do because of your participation in PPO plans, your collection ought to be 100 percent of your production. It's worth mentioning again that you should always use your UCR fees when presenting treatment fees because you can never be 100 percent sure that the patient has coverage on the date of service until you receive their insurance payment. Sometimes employers change insurance plans and the notification email is not read in a timely manner by your patient. To protect yourself from falsely promising a patient a certain write-off amount, it is best to provide them with your UCR fees. Once you calculate their write-off amount based on the insurance plan details provided to you, then you can present this as an estimate of the write-off amount and include a place for the patient to initial. When you figure out what their co-payment is, remember that patients would much rather receive a refund from you instead of a bill to pay more because their insurance did not cover the amount you were led to believe would be covered. So, if you know from past experience that your co-pay estimates for certain insurance plans are off by 20 percent, it is best to add that 20 percent to the co-pay and collect it prior to starting treatment. Remember, it's recommended that you collect more at the beginning of treatment and refund the patient after insurance payment if they have a credit. Better to do it this way than to send a bill because the patient's insurance did not pay you as much as expected after thirty or more days have passed and treatment has been completed.

Let patients know in advance that although you are a PPO provider for their insurance plan, you cannot be in control of or guarantee that payment will be secured in a timely manner. Let them know how long insurance plans legally have to send either payment or notification of not paying and the reason for not paying. Let them know that the insurance coverage and their benefits are an agreement between the patient's employer and the insurance plan and that you have no power to influence what insurance will or will not cover. Your job is to send the claim within X number of days (usually within one to three business days), after providing treatment and include the necessary information to secure payment for the patient. Be very clear about when the patient's insurance claim will be sent out and the length of time that is allowed for receiving this payment. If payment is not received in a timely manner, you will need to contact the insurance company and sometimes the patient so that their HR department can help with securing payment. Usually, insurance plans do not like it when an employer's HR department is alerted for late payments since the employer may choose not to renew their contract for the following year if too many complaints are received from their employees.

If you are not a preferred provider on any insurance plans, your collection policies need to state this clearly. It's important for patients to know how much they will be responsible for paying out of pocket. You can let them know whether you will be billing their insurance for them or not. Not billing a patient's insurance typically means insurance not paying because there is usually so much information that needs to be provided that a patient may not have knowledge of. How you decide whether to accept and bill PPO insurances depends on your ideal patient profile, your values, and the type of practice that you want to have. If you accept PPO insurance plans and want to drop all or a few, it is best to do a comprehensive evaluation to assess whether your practice is in a position to successfully do this or not. Most PPO plans require dentists to provide written notice to the plan and comply with a thirty-day, sixty-day, or even ninety-day notice to the existing patients of the practice. Therefore, knowledge of your contract and a carefully laid-out plan will be necessary to ensure the least amount of disruption for your existing patients. You need to assess whether your practice can survive losing all the existing patients under that plan and not attracting future new patients that have this plan. If only a few patients in your practice have the plan that you want to drop and new patients rarely have this plan, you will face no or minimal disruption. However, if 50 percent of your practice, as well as new patients that call for appointments, are part of the plan you're considering dropping, the disruption to your practice will be catastrophic. If any coach or consultant tells you to drop insurance plans without a careful and thorough evaluation of your practice and an explanation of the impact of this change, please obtain a second opinion.

When you and your team members are very clear about your collection policy, you should have zero to minimal receivables because you collect co-payments on the date of service. You may or may not accept credit cards, or you may offer CareCredit or other financing options. Whatever you choose to do is your choice and can work if your policies are made with your ideal patient profile in mind, your policies are clear and stated in writing, you have systems in place to make it simple for patients to pay you, and you provide them with honest and clear knowledge of your fees and how you manage their insurance. Money is one of those sensitive subjects that needs to be handled carefully because there are many fears associated with money and finances. For a copy of the three forms that can help you with collections (insurance benefits form, co-payment calculation worksheet, financial arrangement sample), please send a request through www.drbitasaleh.com.

Reflection Points

1. Write your collection policy in detail with your ideal patient profile and your values in mind. Once completed, review with all of your team members and make sure they understand with some exercise drills.

2. Prepare an insurance benefits form that corresponds to the codes that you most commonly use in your practice and decide where to place this form for easy accessibility in the patient's chart (if you have paper charts) or in the patient's electronic records (if you're a paperless office).

3. Prepare a co-payment worksheet.

4. Prepare a financial arrangement form and have this form reviewed by a business attorney.

5. Review all these forms with your team members and include how and when each staff member takes part in the completion of each form.

CHAPTER 11:

Delicate Balancing of the Overhead Seesaw

Overhead is the catchall phrase for all the expenses necessary to keep your practice in operation. Remember that, most importantly, you need to pay yourself. Other than that, there are two categories of expenses: direct and indirect. Direct expenses are those such as your rent or, if you own your office suite, the mortgage and taxes owed to the bank and the state for owning land, electricity costs, and more. Usually, direct expenses don't change a lot from month to month whereas indirect expenses do. An example of an indirect expense would be your dental lab bill. This will vary month to month depending on how many procedures you do requiring lab work. It's a well-known fact that dental practices run very high overheads. The reason for that is dental practices operate like a surgery center, requiring expensive x-ray machines and equipment in order to be operational. It's not uncommon for a dental practice to operate at 60 to 80 percent or higher overhead. If a practice can run at 50 percent overhead, that is a very efficiently run practice.

To make wise choices, you need to know what your overhead is. This can be determined by looking at the bills you have paid in the last twelve months using QuickBooks or a similar accounting software or you can ask your bookkeeper or CPA for a list. Fixed costs are ones that you cannot eliminate, but that doesn't mean you cannot negotiate them. Make sure in reviewing your fixed costs that you do everything you can to keep those costs at a minimum. This may mean negotiating regularly with companies like the phone company for the best deals or switching to internet phones instead of using landlines. These are just examples. As with everything else, what you choose to do depends on your practice's needs and what you value. Every service or product has its own pros and cons and you will need to weigh these and decide which ones suit your needs the best based on your values and their affordability.

Your variable overhead costs are expenses that vary instead of being the same each month. One example would be continuing education (CE) costs. You may decide to go to Florida to take a course that is the most expensive CE offered, but you do it because the subject matter is an area of growing interest for you and being an expert in this area will allow you to do your job better. Therefore, if your practice is in another state, the cost of travel (plane and hotel) will need to be factored into the cost of taking this course. On the other hand, to keep your variable overhead cost at a minimum, you may decide to obtain your CE credits by taking the free courses offered as part of your membership at your local dental society.

Many of my clients ask whether they should include CE for their employees and, if they do, are they required to pay that employee their regular hourly rate during their presence in the class? The best way to know what is correct in cases of employees is to contact a labor law attorney. I do not mean a business attorney who can also advise you on labor law; I mean a firm that specializes in and only does labor law. Every state has specific requirements and a labor law attorney can guide you best. Paying for their time to answer your questions is better than the penalties you would pay for not knowing the law.

For CE specifically, a good place to start is deciding whether you are making the training mandatory or not. If you are, it is best to pay them their regular hourly pay as well as costs of travel. However, if it is not mandatory and is on a day that they normally do not work at your office, you can offer to only pay the cost of the course without paying for their time or travel. Whatever you decide has to be first approved by a labor law attorney and stated clearly in your basic office manual that each employee has read and signed. Doing so will remove any doubts and questions for you and your employees.

One aspect of the overhead that is worth special mention here is that an hourly rate is your most expensive overhead. Therefore, automate as much as possible. For example, if there is a program that sends automatic emails and text confirmations to your patients to remind them of their appointments, it is worth it to pay the cost of such automation instead of having to hire someone to do this as part of their job. If this person calls in sick or quits unexpectedly, it will not affect the operation of your business if automatic reminders are in place for patients. The more you can minimize your practice's dependence on hourly employees, the more efficiently your office will run in their absence.

Circling back to CE, choose wisely when deciding which continuing education classes are best for you. If the course allows you to gain more knowledge and deliver better dentistry more efficiently, don't take that for granted. Once the course is over, dentists often forget about their new training soon after returning to their office, despite their best intentions. Instead, make the time to train your team members if they did not accompany you to the course and start implementing what you learned. Take pictures of the results of the beautiful dentistry that this course made possible and share it with your existing patients and in your marketing efforts. You will soon learn that being a dentist and business owner goes hand in hand with being a good marketer. You're the one who needs to have the confidence to brag and tell stories about how you have helped patients before expecting your team to do the same. Enthusiasm encourages the same whereas modesty and silence result in no one knowing how great you truly are. And all these details factor into your overhead.

Dental and office supplies are another variable overhead cost that you can manage by arranging a group discount from dental suppliers. Many state dental associations offer such discounts, so, as long as you are a member, you may want to take advantage of any discounts offered as part of your membership. If not, you may choose to speak to your colleagues to see if you can form an alliance that can help you get discounts from dental supply companies.

If you are projecting that you will be profitable and required to pay heavy taxes at the end of the year, it is wise to do quarterly projections with your CPA. If there is a piece of equipment that you've had your eye on and would like to have, your CPA is the best person to let you know what tax savings purchasing this equipment will provide for you. So, instead of paying taxes, you can purchase equipment that will help your efficiency and patient care. Since dental equipment is never cheap, it is wise for you to have a system in place to objectively evaluate whether buying the equipment is worth the cost. A few questions that you may wish to include in your objective evaluation are:

1. Will it help with end-of-the-year tax savings?
2. Will it improve the speed and efficiency of delivering treatment?
3. Will it improve quality of treatment?
4. Will it increase patient satisfaction?
5. Will it positively affect patient acceptance of treatment?
6. Is it required by law?
7. Will it help my physical being?
8. Will it only satisfy my ego?

For me, magnification loops and a light were a non-negotiable expense. By helping me see better, they helped me improve the efficiency of delivering high quality dentistry by reducing the amount of time it took to complete treatment. Patient satisfaction improved because patients spent less time in my dental chair with their mouths open. In addition, my physical body thanked me at the end of each day, especially after long appointments when I could not take a break for five or more consecutive hours.

A factor that often remains hidden in the cost of purchasing new equipment is whether you can afford to pay for it all at once or you have to finance it. If you're going to finance it, keep in mind that the monthly payments, as well as the finance charges and fees, will be added to future monthly overhead costs. These are the times when having a good relationship with the bank that you have a business account with is crucial. In my experience, getting an equipment loan or using money from a business line of credit will come at a much lower finance charge than getting an equipment loan from the bank associated with the equipment company. The latter is the option that often comes with hidden embedded fees. Unless you have the contract looked at by an attorney or your CPA, you'll never know they exist until three months into the loan when you're wondering why you're paying so much more than the finance charge presented to you upon signing the loan.

Another important factor to consider when deciding on overhead costs is again your energy and your time as your most valuable resources. Don't ever take this lightly. In your younger years, you may feel that you have an endless supply of energy and get seduced into loving the high after a very productive day where you hardly took a break. But remember, that feeling is just seduction; it's not love. It is the opposite of love and self-care. Being productive is great and necessary but not when it is made possible at the expense of missing your breaks. Keep in mind that you are in this career for the long-term, not just the short-term. Your energy and caring for your body need to be at the top of your list.

For instance, you may be enticed to reduce your overhead by paying your office bills yourself because it may seem so easy to do. This is another trap. You are a doctor, not a bookkeeper. Your energy has to be saved for tasks that only you can do, such as doing dentistry, making connections with your patients, and increasing referrals. Even if you have time to spare to do your own bookkeeping, don't do it. Hire a professional bookkeeper to not only pay your bills but also provide you with weekly, monthly, and yearly reports that help you to see trends in your finances. If you are doing your own bookkeeping, although it may be simple, it will be the biggest waste of time that you will engage in. The wisest decision would be to delegate.

Another important overhead cost worth considering is when to hire an office manager. If you have time in your schedule to do the hygiene but don't have time to keep up with the many required regulations and staff management issues, it would be more beneficial to hire an office manager than a hygienist. Again, it all comes down to what your time and energy are worth. You will be most effective engaged in patient care rather than managing employees or complying with yet another new law that mandates every office test their sterilizers every day, requires employee training, or another similarly time-consuming task.

To make it easier, let's break down your time and energy into numbers. What is your time worth? If your time is worth $400 per hour because that is what is required for you to meet your overhead and salaries, then any task that either directly or indirectly does not bring in money needs to be delegated. Direct patient care at this hourly rate for thirty-two hours per week (four days a week) will bring you $12,800 per week. A single practitioner producing $51,200 per month ($12,800x4) is a decent amount of production. You can then use an extra day each week to do indirect patient marketing, such as giving speeches or participating in community building activities that increase awareness and attract new ideal patients to your practice. Once you are fully booked with direct patient care and are able to maintain this production level for three consecutive months, then it's time to look at adding a hygienist slowly to your practice starting with one day a week. Always stay within your expertise and don't devalue yourself by engaging in activities that do not match your expertise.

One important aspect of keeping your overhead in check is raising your fees each year to match cost of living increases. You will find that your dental and office supplies will increase, your lab bills will increase, and so on. Being prepared for these increases will prevent being caught in an unpleasant surprise. This increase applies to your UCR fees, as well as negotiating yearly fee increases with insurance plans that you are a preferred provider for.

Overhead is a reality of owning a business and learning how to keep it in a manageable state every day is necessary for being successful. Clients always ask me whether they should run their office at 60 percent overhead or 65 percent or whether 70 percent is acceptable. My answer is different for every practice. There is never a moment in time where two practices are exactly the same. A dental practice is not a cookie-cutter business. It's comprised of human beings working together to help other human beings, all of whom have different emotions, thoughts, beliefs, and values. And finding the answer to the question of overhead always begins with asking a lot of other questions.

Reflection Points

1. Prepare a list of overhead costs—both direct and indirect/variable—based on the last twelve months in order to figure out what your overhead is currently.
2. Hire a bookkeeper and request weekly, monthly, and yearly reports and an explanation of trends.
3. Prepare your basic office manual and have it reviewed by a labor law attorney.

4. Have all team members read the office manual and allow them time to ask questions and sign the manual during their regular office hours. Keep this document in the office in an area that is easily accessible to all team members.

5. Cross-train your team members for maximum efficiency.

6. Find a labor law attorney and CPA who are easily accessible for guidance when needed.

CHAPTER 12:

Owning Your Power as the Leader of Your Practice

I n each chapter so far, I have placed emphasis on determining your values, what you find fulfilling in your life, and your boundaries. These truly take center stage in this chapter as you reflect on owning your power as the leader of your practice.

Let's take a look at what owning your power could mean. One time, a client was frazzled when she joined our weekly call. Her hygienist was giving her an ultimatum—again—stating that she needed a raise and if she didn't get one, she would have to find another job. During our discussion, I realized that this hygienist has been asking for a raise every six months and currently her salary was the same as that of a dentist performing dental treatment. In addition, my client shared that she had a long and close friendship with her hygienist, which made it even harder to say no and set boundaries. She was rightfully spinning with anxiety. On the one hand, she couldn't afford to pay the hygienist more since she was already getting paid very well. But on the other hand, she couldn't be without a hygienist and didn't want to lose their friendship because it was a source of great emotional support for her. One can only imagine how her day was going! This kind of disruption is very common. Employees will hold the dentist hostage for increased pay, threatening to leave if they don't get their desired pay increase. The correct word that describes this behavior is extortion: the practice of obtaining something of benefit (such as money) through force or threats. I'm always surprised when employees who take part in such activity view it as negotiation, but it's not important to get into the psychology or the minds of employees here. What is important for a dentist is digging deep to identify their values and what fulfills them in their work life. When this is discovered and written down, your boundaries fall into place very quickly. It quickly became very clear to my client that friendship does not include distortion and by befriending an employee, the boundaries of their employer/employee relationship became very fuzzy. Complying with such demands sends the wrong message to other team members who then become resentful and lose respect for you as a leader.

Every dentist I know despises employee problems. They often wish they could just walk into their office, treat patients, and leave at the end of the day with money in their pocket for the dentistry they performed. That is a nice fantasy, but as a business owner, you are the leader. You need to lead and sometimes make tough decisions, but it does not have to be tough all the time. Every business should have systems and procedures in place so that employees are clear about what is expected of them. They need to know what their job entails and so much more.

Once you have written down and become clear on what your values are and what you find fulfilling, you will find that your boundaries really do fall into place very quickly. It's also valuable to recognize what circumstances and situations test you and result in you not honoring your word or values. Working on these with your coach and/or consultant helps you identify these situations and have solutions ready for the places that trip you up. For example, my client mentioned above had abandonment issues since childhood. When someone in her tribe threatened to leave for more pay, she would get triggered and succumb to their demand because she viewed a member of her tribe leaving the same as being left alone to die. It was a traumatic event for her. Once she became clear that she didn't value being extorted, we worked together to compile a detailed action plan for when an employee leaves so that her discomfort would be minimal to none. Part of this plan was to establish a professional relationship with a temp agency that she trusted so that if anyone on her team left, with one phone call to this agency, she could have the position filled temporarily until she found a permanent replacement. Losing a key employee is disrupting, but being prepared and having systems and policies in place can make the disruption minimal to nothing.

Along those lines, correctly hiring the right employees for your practice is key. It is also one of the most difficult jobs for most dentists. Even when you have done everything you possibly can to hire correctly, you may find that you hired the wrong person after they have worked for you for a period of time. Some people are professional interviewees and are good at painting a picture of being your ideal employee. On the other hand, there are ideal employees who are terrible when interviewed. So, don't completely base your hiring on the interview. This is one area where trusting your intuition will serve you very well. View hiring an employee as a process based on your clearly defined values. A colleague once said to me, "We're so desperate to hire someone that we'll even accept ex-cons." What this statement meant was that he would hire an ex-con because he had been forced into a position where his values were reduced to just having a warm body, regardless of a negative history. It's similar to not planning your meals and waiting to decide what to eat when you're starving. At the point of starvation, you will not choose healthy options because you're likely to grab anything that's easily accessible. That may be french fries or a piece of chocolate, but it won't be a balanced meal.

Begin by writing a detailed job description for each position in your office. When doing this, don't let perfectionism get in the way of finishing them. Write what you know, and, in time, you can add or subtract. This at least gives you a blueprint of a written job description. If you have an employee who is currently in that position and is doing a good job, you can ask them to write the job description. Then you can review it and modify as you see fit.

When you're clear about your values and boundaries, as well as the job description for the person you are looking to hire, it will be much easier to write the content of an advertisement when you need to fill that position. In addition, have a plan for where you will place your ad and what it will cost. Having a short list of questions to ask applicants will deter people who are not serious from applying. Review the resumes that you receive carefully and know in advance which trends in employment are deal-breakers for you. You may decide that a gap in employment or a certain employer who can't be contacted or the person changing jobs every year or two are red flags. Regardless of the reason, pay attention to these red flags. If you have an office manager, you may decide that the office manager reviews all applications and resumes as an initial screening and will bring only the five-star candidates to your attention. It's important that whoever is designated to do this job has time and knows what to look for. For example, if you've asked for three professional employers as references and the applicant gives you three colleagues, you will quickly discover that this person does not follow instructions well. Once you decide to do the interviews, it's best to do all of them in one day. Doing all in one day has many advantages over spreading them out over a long period of time. If any candidate dictates to you the time that they are available and tries to negotiate the time of their interview, know that they are not serious about finding a job.

Have a system for your interview and invite your coach or consultant to be present when you interview. Having an additional person present who is experienced in interviewing will ensure that you run on time and can help with an objective assessment of the person interviewed. During the interview, ask open-ended questions, not yes-or-no questions. People reveal their true nature when answering open-ended questions. I would also recommend adding scenario questions with an ethical dilemma and asking the candidate how they would handle the situation to test their ethical standards. In addition, include simple tasks that test their skills. If you're looking for someone who can write letters and can type fast, you can give them a paragraph or page to type during a timed period and then evaluate their typing for speed and accuracy. If you're hiring a registered dental assistant, you might give them various instruments and ask them to choose the correct ones for a certain procedure in a determined amount of time. This will enable you to assess their basic knowledge and whether or not they know their instruments.

One thing I highly recommend that you stay away from is making a decision before you go through the entire interview process. Remember that you have chosen an interview process because each step provides valuable information, so don't prematurely decide that someone is right for the job until you have completed the entire process. Let the candidate know at the end of the interview that you'll be calling their references. You want to be sure the references know they will be called so they can make themselves available to receive a call from you. Most people have caller ID on their phones and if they don't recognize your number, they will not answer. It may take days or weeks for them to check their voicemail. It will negatively impact the candidate if you can't reach their references. Also, make sure the candidate has given you the correct phone numbers to call. If you hear that the doctor they worked for has moved or died or is no longer practicing, they need to give you the contact info for another reference. Check references for seven years of employment and do a detailed background check on the applicant who has completed the interview successfully and you are considering for employment. I can't stress the importance of this enough. Finding an employee you can trust is similar to finding a babysitter for your six-month-old infant who will be in your house caring for your child when no one else is present. In the same way that you wouldn't allow someone incompetent to care for your child, you shouldn't allow someone you're not sure about to become your employee.

Even when you have hired someone, the first ninety days of their employment should be a time for you to assess whether they are actually suitable for employment. During this time, continue the same hiring methods until after their first ninety days have passed and certainly do not give them your office keys or the passcode to the office alarm system during this time as it sends the wrong message about what is supposed to be a probationary period. Do everything to help them succeed, but do not become emotionally attached to the idea that this is it and you have found the right employee until you see the proof. I have been in situations where a candidate presented themselves so well that I was 100 percent convinced they were the right candidate. However, when they started their job, there were certain things they would do that were so wrong (things that would be part of not just their job but their character) that I would end up experiencing cognitive dissonance. This is when what you thought someone was like turns out to be so opposite of what you expected that your mind cannot accept the reality of who they truly are. This is another reason why it's valuable to have someone such as a coach or consultant helping you with your hiring decisions.

When you check references during the hiring process, be sure to have a number of questions written down to ask. Do not ask a reference to comment on whether they liked the applicant or not. In addition, asking generalized, open-ended questions will only invite subjective responses that may not be of value for you. You don't want to take up too much of the person's time, but you do want to make a connection so that you can obtain true answers. First and foremost, you want to verify the dates of employment and the hourly salary, as well as whether the reference was the employer or not. I usually give my clients a short list of valuable questions to ask, but you must know that many people may not want to say anything negative so they will just say the minimum required. It's important that you are trained to read between the lines and carefully evaluate what a reference says. As an example, one of my clients had an experience with calling references during the hiring process that actually prompted him to hire me as his coach and consultant. He was looking to hire a receptionist for his front office, but all his attempts to find a presentable and responsible receptionist had failed. He shared his experience candidly. He had called an employer of a potential candidate who had performed extremely well in her interview to ask him a few questions. When he asked the employer, "Would you hire this person again?" the previous employer responded, "Of course I would. She is very nice and well-mannered, but at that time in her life, she was going through some challenges that caused her to miss work a lot, but that was a long time ago and I'm sure she's worked through that by now because she was always very responsible."

Being new to the hiring process, my client didn't press the previous employer to clarify what those challenges were. He did not see the red flags nor did he read between the lines. He did diligently ask the candidate if there were any challenges currently present that would prevent her to show up to work as required and she said, "No." So, he enthusiastically hired her. Within a few short weeks, he walked into his office one day and one of his dental assistants, after greeting him, announced that he had a patient in room 1 ready to start treatment and his newly hired receptionist in room 2 because she was having panic attacks. It turned out that the panic attacks were a common occurrence for her and one of the reasons that she couldn't maintain a job for a lengthy period of time, which explained the gaps in her employment history. My client made every effort to help this employee, but his efforts were unsuccessful.

She finally resigned and was able to go on disability. This example shows the likelihood of someone being able to present themselves well during the interview but turning out not to be the ideal candidate. Integrity was a value that my client was not willing to compromise. Within a few months of working together, he was able to hire a receptionist who shared similar values and she is still employed by him to this day.

If during the interview a candidate criticizes their previous employer and/or accepts no responsibility for their own actions, know you will also be dealing with that if you hire this individual—someone who will question you and covertly work against you. An example of this would be an employee who uses her time with a patient to talk about herself and her life instead of listening to the patient and doing her job quickly so that the patient's time is not wasted. When this employee takes thirty minutes to clean the temporary cement around a temporary crown when only five minutes is needed to complete this task, she is wasting not only the patient's time but the office's time as well. When corrected on her behavior, she might say that her sharing stories about her grandson helped the patient relax and blame the patient for asking about her grandchildren. She might say that she didn't want to be rude and not answer the patient's questions. The dentist will use valuable office time to train her. She will receive training on how to be polite and answer patient's questions while understanding that although patients are sweet and ask us about our lives, a short answer and diverting the focus of the appointment back to them is more important and effective than taking up extra time sharing about herself. By placing her focus on herself and her story, she has proven time and time again that she slows down and makes mistakes and forgets that the focus of the appointment needs to be on the patient and not her. This team member is repeatedly in listening level I rather than II and III. At this patient's next appointment, this employee might tell the patient, "I got into trouble last time when I told you about my grandson. Doctor gets mad at me when I chat with patients, so I won't be able to talk to you this time." You can imagine the negative impact of these words on the patient.

This is an example of an employee being covertly hostile toward the doctor. The doctor will then remember that during her interview she said that at her last job her employer made her do certain tasks that were not covered under her licensure and would get mad at her when she asked him for help. Now the doctor will fully understand and have evidence of how damaging this employee can be by twisting the truth. But this is only possible if the doctor hears the conversation that this employee had with the patient. It would be most damaging if the doctor never hears about it and conversations such as this continue to go on with other patients and other employees. Soon, patients start to cancel appointments because they don't want to be in a negative environment, employees start to fight amongst themselves, and you may even lose one of your better employees without an explanation. Whenever your office takes a downward spin, there is most often a bad apple in the group who belongs to that 20 percent that causes 80 percent of the problems. This is just one example of why it is so important to have the knowledge and the expertise to know how to pay attention and read between the lines during not just the interview, but the whole hiring process.

The statistic that 20 percent of the population is responsible for 80 percent of problems makes sense. I've found that close to 80 percent of the problems in a dental office are caused by 20 percent of employees. I hope knowing this will bring you some comfort. You're not the only office experiencing problems with employees, and I hope you can rest assured that there are many steps you can take to minimize the damage that can be caused by bad apples. With my help, my clients often find employees who are skilled, honest, responsible, caring, and loyal. As with anything else, doing so requires knowing how to go about finding these gems. To review every single step required for finding and keeping good employees would require another book dedicated to the topic. I do include a program and training specific to this topic in my coaching and consulting, but considering the limited space available in this chapter, I can just give you a few more foundational steps that will help you find and keep the right team members.

1. Identify your values, your boundaries, and what you find fulfilling in your work life, which is the same as your life in general.
2. Hire an attorney who is part of a firm that specializes and only does labor law. Be sure to have them review your job descriptions and your basic office policy manual.
3. Based on the above, write an ad for the position you're looking to hire for and identify the best platform to advertise on. Make this ad simple and concise.
4. Write out a typical daily flow for each position in your office.
5. Obtain agreements from each team member by having them read, ask questions about, and sign their job descriptions, the basic office policy manual, and anything else that is a requirement for their job.
6. Each employee will need to know how they are accountable for their job duties and goals in a way that

is measurable. These measures need to be discussed at certain intervals (yearly, semi-yearly, or quarterly at your discretion).

7. Address how (which conditions need to be met), when, and in what amount a raise will be considered for each employee.

8. Mandate privacy for employment-related discussions with each employee.

9. If you can use automated software to do a certain job, do so.

10. Have and train your employees on a certain communication policy that is required in your office. For example, any problems that are noted need to be presented to the doctor or office manager in writing within twenty-four hours of knowledge of the problem. In addition to presenting the details of the problem, employees must offer at least one reasonable solution with carefully thought-out specifics. That communication will be investigated and replied to within seven days. To receive a sample of this form, please go to www.drbitasaleh.com and request the inter-office communication form.

11. Do yearly ethics training in your office. Consider this as important as the privacy or OSHA trainings that you're required to do by law.

12. Maintain proper employer/employee relationships by being clear and honoring your boundaries. To obtain ongoing support, hire a professional coach and/or consultant who can provide you the support you need on an ongoing basis, not just when things spin out of control.

13. Hire employees mostly based on having and performing their job with values similar to yours instead of hiring those who are more experienced. You can teach skills, but you cannot teach values.

14. Your hiring process needs to be written by you in such detail that if there are any changes in employees, the hiring process can occur with minimum operational challenges.

15. Take the time to learn your dental software better than anyone else in your office. Designate who on your team will have access to which parts of the software. For example, your front office can print daily reports as part of their job, but they should not have access to modify anything once it is entered. No one on your team should be able to enter write-offs in a patient's account, regardless of the nature of the write-off (insurance write-off or patient discount).

16. Review the daily report that your computer generates. This includes all activity for that day, including procedure codes for production, collection, and write-offs. A daily report should include everything that you need to know about the operation of your practice. With most dental software, daily reports can be customized to your needs. Be sure to close out the day after you have reviewed the report.

17. Check audit reports daily. Audit reports will show if any changes were made and by whom before closing out the day.

18. As part of establishing and maintaining security, you as the administrator can assign accessibility of certain tasks to only a certain group. For example, you can make sure

no group other than the administrator has the clearance to make changes after the daily close-out. Therefore, an assistant belonging to the back office group cannot go into Mr. Smith's account the day after Mr. Smith's treatment and add or subtract a procedure code. In the same token, your receptionist belonging to the front office group cannot go into Mr. Smith's account the day after his treatment and delete a cash payment he made.

19. Have systems in place to train your employees and empower them, but never ever let anyone hold you hostage in your practice. Write in your basic office policy (in language that your labor law attorney approves of and is easily understood by a layperson) that if any employee threatens to leave in order to secure a raise, they understand that doing so will clearly imply a verbal notice of their resignation and allow them to leave right away with no further negotiation or discussion.

20. Have available in writing in your basic office policy what kind of measurable behavior and outcomes on your employees' part leads to consideration for a raise. If you are offering bonuses, be sure to be very clear about the amount and the conditions under which a bonus is offered. When you offer a bonus, offer it to everyone, not just to one particular group of employees. You want to create a culture where your employees are encouraged to work together as a team while always respecting you as their leader. As part of their training, include subjects such as communication, conflict resolution, or teamwork in addition to improving their primary job skills.

As dentists, you're expected to do your job extremely well on patients who mostly suffer from varying degrees of fear and anxiety around dental treatment. That alone takes its toll on you. The nature of your profession requires a lot from you without you having to deal with employee problems. I invite you to really take this in and value what you have to do on a daily basis just to show up and be at your best for your patients. There will never be a staff member who knows more than you about patient care or what is right for your practice. So, never turn to your staff or rely on them to tell you what to do. Surround yourself with and foster only those humans whose sole intention for being a part of your team is to support you and your relationship with your patients. Once you find these exceptional humans, nourish and foster their growth and well-being by being the type of leader who leads effectively. Keep in mind that no one is born knowing how to be an effective leader. Just like any other skill, effective leadership can be learned. You may be in the top 1 percent of dentists who have the skills to perform the best that dentistry has to offer, but competency alone does not automatically imply that you are an effective leader. Unfortunately, in the current climate, most continuing education courses are centered around honing your skills in dentistry alone, which, although necessary, is insufficient for a business owner. In addition to developing your skills in dentistry, there is a great deal of value in taking courses that develop your skills in, for example, sales, communication, or leadership.

Honor the hard work that allows you the privilege of owning and operating a dental practice and know that being an effective leader begins with self-awareness and reflecting on your own emotions and wounds that may cause you to be triggered.

Great leadership is revealed in how you show up for yourself, your patients, and your team beyond your skills, capability, and confidence as a dentist. Effective leadership starts with our connection to the deepest parts of ourselves, including vision, courage, fearlessness, compassion, collaboration, purposefulness, humility, and much more.

In the same way that you worked so hard and were committed to becoming a great dentist, you can learn how to become a great leader. However you go about getting there, I encourage you not to ever give your power away by inadvertently hiring the kind of person who gives themselves permission—unbeknownst to you—to perform fraud or embezzle from you or even stalk you and break and enter into your home. These unfortunate incidents happen more often than we would like in our profession, and the damage to the business owner is real. Just like your house, your office needs to be a safe space where you can do your job of helping patients heal and get healthy without the added worry of managing problems caused by employees who should never have made it successfully through the interview process.

Reflection Points

1. What does owning your power mean to you? What is the significance of it?
2. Write job descriptions for three key employees in your practice including yourself.
3. Describe one time where you gave your power away. Describe how that affected you? What were you afraid would happen if you stood in your power instead of giving it away?

CHAPTER 13:

Surrender Energetic Leaks for Maximum Efficiency

Let's start with a simple definition of an energetic leak. An energetic leak is anything that inwardly or outwardly occupies space in our mind and hinders or slows down our forward flow. When we're expending energy in ways that cause an energy deficit, a wise leader will have enough self-awareness to recognize that an energy leak exists and take the time to stop, surrender, lean in to the deeper lessons, and repair the energy leak.

Saying "yes" when we really want and need to say "no" is a common way that we dentists open ourselves to an energy leak. Any incomplete task or to-do item, idea, or memory that drains your energy when you think of it or see it—even to a small degree—can cause energy leaks. An example could be forgetting to tell your assistant to do a better job setting up for procedures. If this is not addressed, the next time your assistant doesn't properly set up for a procedure the energy leak will increase as you get more frustrated because you didn't take the time to bring it up with her the first time you noticed it. Another example is wanting to send thank you notes to your referral sources for referring patients but you've run out of thank you cards and you have not had time to get new ones.

We're conditioned to constantly do things that produce money. I once heard one of my colleagues say that she trained herself to ask each time she started a task whether this task would generate immediate money for her. If it did, she would continue the task and if not, she would stop. I don't know how that worked out for her in the long-term, but the lesson is that it's vital to our well-being to stop once in a while and check in with ourselves to see how we feel when we're just in *being* mode instead of *doing* mode. This is when we can become aware of energetic leaks and can take the time and the necessary steps to end them.

In this chapter, I'll touch on preventing the most common sources of energetic leaks in a dental practice. One of the most common energetic leaks is a constant worry when dentists don't know if they will meet their production or collection numbers each month. Not having any power over this can cause unnecessary anxiety, which lowers your energy and adversely affects your success rate when presenting treatment recommendations to patients. To prevent this from occurring, make time to monitor the pulse and heartbeat of your practice in regular weekly intervals. Start by evaluating where you are currently and set goals to determine where you want and need to be on a weekly basis. Once you know where you are and where you need to be, you can decide what action steps are needed to get you to your goal. You can look back on prior months when you reached your goals to see what occurred that month that enabled your success. For example, you may discover that, looking at your last six months, May was your best month. By looking deeper into that month, you may realize that you did twenty veneers on one patient (in addition to other work) and that is what led you to meeting your monthly production and collection goals. You can look even deeper and find out what led to this patient deciding to get her veneers completed in that month. You may realize that she was getting a divorce from her husband and wanted him to pay for the veneers before the divorce was finalized. Knowing this will help you concentrate your efforts on attracting more patients like her and establishing yourself as *the* cosmetic dentist in your neighborhood. She will then become your ideal patient.

Many dentists do not take vacations because they are afraid that being away for a week will affect their production numbers. If you look at previous months, you may find that the month before going on vacation, you were more productive than any other month so that the increased production compensated for the week that you were on vacation. Reflecting on this will allow you to let go and surrender the old belief that "I can't afford to go on vacation" to the new belief that "going on vacation every three months is necessary to consistently meet quarterly goals." Once you have accumulated a list of what works and what doesn't work, you no longer need to worry because you have actionable steps that are proven to work for you and can be repeated month after month.

Another valuable evaluation is to check in with yourself at the beginning of each week to see if you have enough scheduled production to meet your weekly goals. If you find that you don't have enough scheduled production, you can right away add one of the action steps from the list of what has worked well in the past, to ensure meeting your goals before the end of the week.

The same steps can be taken for marketing. At first, you may not know what kind of marketing efforts will bring in new patients, and you won't know until you try out a strategy and measure the results. What worked for me when I was practicing was to speak in front of an audience. I was not afraid of public speaking, and I was able to make connections with the audience and establish trust quickly. This was the best way for me to attract new patients to my practice. I had an entire policy around this one marketing effort that included the number of people in the audience, the proximity of the venue to the office, what time of the day this would happen, whether or not I would cater a meal, and, if I was speaking in front of the employees of a company, I would find out what dental insurance they carried and whether I was a PPO provider for that insurance plan. I also looked at whether those employees were in an age group that corresponded to my ideal patient's age group, along with other factors. The purpose of marketing is to bring new ideal patients to your practice, not to market to whoever wherever in the hope of attracting everyone, which ultimately means attracting no one.

Evaluating numbers from your past can help you gain much-needed information about which efforts work and which ones don't. Once you know this, you can do more of what works, drop what doesn't, and get rid of the energy leak coming from worrying about your production or marketing.

Let's look at another example of an energy leak that negatively affected production. One of my clients was a dentist who noticed that for the past twenty years in his practice, the month of August had consistently been his most productive month. He hired a new receptionist in February and had noticed that his production had decreased since he hired her. This was a source of an energy leak for him because it occupied his mind and he had no answers about why this was occurring. He and the rest of his team were doing their jobs the same as before. The only thing that had changed in his office was this receptionist. When August came and went, he became alarmed. Never in the past twenty years had he not exceeded his goals in August, but that year, his low production had continued.

When he hired me in September, he was rightfully experiencing panic, which wasn't helping the situation. A careful review of his practice showed that he was right. In the last twenty years, he had consistently exceeded his goals every August until that year. As a practice owner, you always have a gut feeling when something doesn't feel right. This doctor, although he liked the new receptionist, knew all along that something was off and that it was contributing to the decline of production in his practice.

Within a few days of interviewing all of his team members, it was discovered that this receptionist had divorced her abusive ex-husband who had promised her that he would find her and take their son away from her. She had since remarried, but she changed jobs frequently because she was so afraid that he would find her. Each time the office phone rang, or the door opened, she was afraid that it would be her ex-husband. Fear was written all over her face and she froze whenever she had to answer the phone or greet someone. She would have been much happier if she was in a secluded room in the back of the office where no one could see her and could do insurance all day. I hate to think that anyone could be energetically powerful enough to disrupt an office in this way, but the numbers spoke for themselves.

Since the office did not have such a position to offer her, she left to join another practice that could offer a room in the back where she could hide. Within one month of her leaving, the office's production returned to what it used to be and continued to improve. The fear that this receptionist had felt had spread through the office and affected everyone, including the patients, other team members, and the doctor. To prevent this from happening again, we went back and looked at the office's numbers for the previous two years and found a lot of valuable information. Patterns were found, goals were set, and action steps were put into place. These plans were shared with everyone on his team so that they could also look for and notice strange occurrences. Everyone shared the same goals and was committed to expansion rather than elimination or shrinkage and the practice was literally saved. Fortunately, the doctor was willing to lean into the deeper lessons that he learned during this unfortunate time. He often now jokes and says, "If this hadn't happened, I would have never felt the need to hire someone like you." He is grateful that he finally listened to his intuition that something was drastically wrong in his practice.

Unfortunately, the culture of our profession looks down upon asking for help and views it as weakness. Dentists get together and brag about their practices and how much money they're making to save face when inside they're suffering and feeling ashamed that they don't know how to solve all the problems in their practice on their own. Somehow, the belief that they should do everything in isolation is ingrained in them so deeply that asking a professional coach or consultant for help seems equivalent to claiming defeat or admitting that they're not enough.

Really, it's the opposite. It requires a great deal of courage and sensibility to recognize that your job is to do dentistry and take care of your patients, so you cannot be everywhere at once keeping an eye on every aspect of your practice. Speaking from experience, please believe me when I say that learning is much harder when you do it on your own and have to learn from your mistakes than when you hire a certified professional business coach and/or consultant who has been though what you're going through and has the knowledge to guide you away from the majority of mistakes.

Reflection Points

Below are a few examples of some of the most common situations that can cause energetic leaks. Do everything in your power to have policies in place to minimize or eliminate the negative effect of energetic leaks caused by things on—or similar to—the list below.

1. A patient announcing that they are leaving the practice and want their records.
2. Patients showing up late, causing you to run late for your next patient.
3. Patients no-showing for their appointments and wasting valuable time when another patient could have been seen.
4. A restoration not fitting well on a tooth because of any number of reasons and you having to send the restoration back to the lab for a remake.
5. Not being prepared for lab fee increases.
6. Patients not scheduling for recommended treatment.

7. An employee leaving, being fired, calling in sick, or showing up late to work.
8. Arguments, bickering, and gossip amongst team members.
9. Covertly hostile employees.
10. Patients with dental fear and anxiety.
11. Patients who have to be turned over to a collection agency due to non-payment.
12. Employees not complying with or challenging your policies.
13. Insurance fraud.
14. Prescription fraud.
15. Employee embezzlement.
16. Employee stalking.
17. Employee using your office resources for their personal needs.

CHAPTER 14:

Practice Radical Self-care without Guilt

As a dentist and business owner, you are called every day to face challenges that are daunting for any business owner. In addition, you are the only one who has the expertise and the license to practice dentistry. Even hygienists cannot practice without varying levels of supervision by a dentist. Your full presence is required for your office to operate and generate money; yet, most dentists do not give themselves permission to radically care for themselves. Radical self-care does not just mean getting eight hours of sleep a night and eating healthy. In addition to these basics, there is a whole host of self-care measures that I insist on if you are in this profession for the long-term.

You may have started practicing dentistry when you were young, but, every decade, your mental, emotional, and physical health will change in ways that you can't foresee. Nature doesn't allow us to have the wisdom that we have in our sixties in our twenties and the body and the energy that we had in our twenties in our sixties. The best we can do is to prepare and adjust before a stress-related illness stops us in our tracks. Every day that we are at our best is a day that we can take care of ourselves and each other to prevent burnout, addiction, thoughts of suicide, or mental illness. Isolating ourselves in our individual practices and showing a brave face to the rest of the world if we are crumbling inside doesn't serve anyone. You will be called to handle many curveballs in the day-to-day events of your business and practice. If you're not at your best during these times, the accumulation of stress in your life may take you down in one way or another. So, let's talk about radical self-care as something that must be a daily priority (not just in your head but also on your calendar) and not something that is negotiable.

It's my hope that this chapter highlights the importance of and the many varied ways to practice radical self-care.

The first step is to understand the value of asking for help, regardless of where you are in your dental practice, and to be willing to receive help so that you no longer carry the weight of every responsibility you have on your own. When you get clear about what you value in life, it will become much easier to say "no" when you're faced with requests or demands or situations when you know that if you say "yes," you will not be living in accordance with your values. In fact, saying "yes" when you want to say "no" is an act of self-betrayal. Even once you make your needs a priority and set policies in your practice to honor these priorities, you may still feel guilty when you see the disappointed reactions on other people's faces. For example, patients may be disappointed when you no longer offer appointment times during their lunch hour. A lifetime habit of pleasing others will not change overnight, but it can change gradually with support from a certified professional coach. Realizing your values and setting boundaries is a great start but keeping those boundaries requires continuous commitment. Let me put it this way: If you have ever visualized running away to the most remote place in the world where no one can find you, you are in need of some seriously past-due self-care.

Every dentist knows the feeling of completing a productive day of treating patients and exceeding production goals. There is an intoxicating feeling of pleasure that comes from helping care for people and feeling that we are in demand and needed. I know that feeling too well. I have also sacrificed many times, missing lunch and working nonstop all day into the evening. The truth is that this feeling of intoxication from nonstop work can and will rob you of your life.

People who are in this profession love to take care of others. Working hard is a way of life for most of you. So, recognizing the value of changing this behavior may be harder than you realize. Changing a behavior when you have the choice is a lot easier than when you're forced to do it because your career is coming to an early halt due to a stress-related illness or any number of reasons. Women dentists are often torn between managing their career and their family, or they choose not to get married so they can put their career first. Men are expected to provide a certain lifestyle and shoulder much of the responsibility. Both genders are conditioned to keep their chins up and pretend they are so noble that they are not touched by life's stresses. What they don't realize until it's too late is that life happens to all of us, regardless of how noble or generous we are.

Radical self-care is about basing every decision on choices that not only sustain you but are nurturing, such as making sure that your practice nourishes you instead of sucking all your energy out of you, not making commitments based on guilt or fear of appearing selfish, and, most importantly, getting yourself to a point financially where you get to choose how many hours or years you work.

When your head is filled with thoughts, which tends to be the norm, it's impossible to know whether the decisions you're making are based in fear or love. Decisions made out of fear are mostly reactive and are made with the intention of avoiding the object of our fear. When our mind is quiet and we're connected to our heart, the decisions we make will be based on inspiration and empowerment.

As I described earlier, meditation had a profoundly positive effect on my level of stress, which had caused ongoing migraines for me. Meditation allows you to consciously begin and end your day so that you don't bring stress from work home. Mindfulness Meditation allows you to practice focusing your awareness in the present moment, and Transcendental Meditation allows you to quiet your mind by transcending all thought. A great deal of research has been done on meditation, and it's been shown to be effective for reducing anxiety, depression, overwhelm, PTSD, and migraines. Those who practice meditation regularly experience increased levels of functioning in various aspects of their life, not just in their thinking processes. They report better physical health and well-being, greater ability to concentrate, and increased creativity as some of the benefits of meditation, which all contribute to making decisions based on love.

There are many meditation techniques available. Some people find it difficult to sit in one place for a period of time without doing something. For these people, walking silently and mindfully is a form of meditation. The speed at which you walk is irrelevant. The important aspect of this type of mindfulness meditation is becoming aware of the present moment. Guided visualization is another meditation technique widely available on the internet, especially on YouTube. Regulating and watching your breath or intentionally listening to sounds or music are a couple other ways of meditating.

Your basic character and current needs determine which method of meditation works best for you. If you are experiencing a crisis, calming your thoughts by counting your breaths while breathing regularly will calm your body. A walking or moving meditation can be effective if you are unable to sit still. If you wish to reduce the chatter in your mind, a mantra meditation may be useful. This type of meditation sets up a rhythmic entrainment in your mind that brings harmony to your thoughts and actions. If your priority is to cleanse yourself of stress before arriving home at the end of a workday, running energy through the body (similar to taking a shower in sensation and light) and grounding negative thoughts and feelings to the earth might prove to be the best method of meditation.

Our thoughts often keep us engaged in repetitive patterns and limiting beliefs. By quieting our minds, meditation allows us to access a deeper wisdom, a deeper state of consciousness. As we silence the mind, we open up to disengaging our habitual responses (fear, anger, resentment, or judgment) and freeing ourselves from patterns that don't serve us.

Another form of self-care is clearing your emotional wounds. If something that a patient says has the power to trigger negative emotions within you, it is worth taking a look at and resolving the source of that emotional wound. For example, you may have lost a beloved pet when you were young and that was a very painful experience for you. Many families don't know how to deal with grief and believe in not sharing negative feelings and emotions as a way to move forward in life. But those feelings don't go away. They get suppressed and, much like filing a book in a library, they are placed in a bank of memories in our brains, ready to be recalled at the first sign of a word or sentence that reminds us of our original loss—and every other loss thereafter. When triggered, all those negative feelings return as if the loss just happened. It's important to hire a therapist or professional coach who is trained to witness your feelings and process your grief and loss. Not only is this important for you, but it's also vital because most of the patients who seek your help are fearful of dental treatment and you may be the only one who can help them get through the appointment successfully—a task made much harder if you end up getting triggered yourself.

Positive and high-quality social support is also exceptionally important for maintaining physical and psychological health. I encourage you to examine the quality of your interactions with those whom you spend your free time with. If you have six hours a week to spend time socializing and that time is spent with family, friends, colleagues, or neighbors who engage in negative gossip or covertly stab you in the back by barraging you with insensitive and inappropriate comments, you will be more stressed at home and less resilient to the stresses at work. Surround yourself with people who actively support you in positive ways during times of both wellness and crisis. The quality of your relationships is just as important as the quantity.

Taking care of your physical body might seem to be a given, but most of the time, as I mentioned earlier, dentists get so wrapped up in working hard that they oversee this vitally important aspect of their health. As obvious as it may seem, I cannot ignore mentioning it here. Have a balanced and nourishing diet and take the time to eat with awareness. I know many dentists who eat their lunch in five minutes in between seeing patients or spend most of their lunch break driving to and waiting in line to get a sandwich, only to eat in their car while driving back to their office. Eating is not just about shoving food in your mouth and swallowing so that the hunger signals are turned off. Eating with awareness invites nurturing energy because you signal to your body that you're taking care of it, that you're actively taking part in nurturing yourself.

Along with a balanced and nourishing diet, exercise regularly as well, not just for your heart's health but to build strength and resilience. For me, I knew that the only way that I could avoid back and neck problems was to strengthen my core muscles. By paying attention to your body, you will also recognize what areas require strengthening. However, keeping the exercises varied will help you in the long run. In your younger years, you may be able to do a lot of high-impact aerobic activity, such as basketball or kickboxing, but as your body ages, you may find that your knees start to hurt and you will be forced to switch to yoga instead, for example. It is always harder to make decisions based on having to rather than choosing to. If you already have been partaking in a regular yoga practice, you'll find it to be an easier transition than if you have never considered yoga before or, even worse, if you hold a belief that yoga is a middle-age activity!

I also would be remiss not to mention sleep. Get a good night's sleep. This means getting enough sleep to feel completely rested. When you're in your thirties, you might be fully rested with six hours of sleep whereas in your fifties you might need eight to nine hours of sleep to be at your best during the day. If you're someone who dreams a lot, you may decide to join a group where dream interpretation is discussed as a self-care add-on.

Minimize or eliminate intoxicants such as alcohol and pay close attention to what causes discomfort in your body. I found that I became extremely sensitive to the smell of chemicals like perfume or cologne or anything that was chemically scented, even hairspray. This was one of the triggers for my migraines, and I had to come to terms with the fact that I had to make some changes in my policies to let my employees and patients know so they could help me stay healthy. Being in a profession where we are used to always taking care of others, it was very hard to admit that I now needed help. I had to draw hard boundaries to honor my own health by refusing to see the few patients who didn't comply even after being informed multiple times.

Acting early to assess and seek treatment for new potential problems requires the kind of self-awareness that springs from kindness and compassion toward yourself. Grounding and chakra cleansing meditations are two of my most favorite meditations for connecting the body to the earth and into full presence in the moment as well as identifying and correcting the energetic disturbances in chakras preceding physical disease. Although it's not in the scope of this book to go into detail about the method of these meditations, they are taught in my coaching program. It's worth mentioning that they can be done quickly and effectively for yourself, your patients, and your team members.

Compassion and loving-kindness cannot be extended to others unless it's first extended to ourselves. Compassion means being fully present in sadness or sympathy while witnessing your own or another's suffering. Our ability to have compassion for others is directly dependent on our ability to be in touch with our own yearnings and pain. Empaths are usually able to feel other people's pain and suffering as though it were their own, but if you're not an empath, it is often through experiencing your own pain that you will open up to a deeper understanding of another's suffering. Compassion doesn't mean that you need to fix the source of suffering, but it is important to offer compassion, especially when you can't fix anything. Compassion requires us to quietly hold space for change to occur, "providing both the stability of a container and the freedom of release,"(244) as Anodea Judith (2004) states.[29] When patients come to our office, our job is to offer solutions for their dental problems. However, sometimes it's more important to offer compassion before offering solutions, and especially when the solution has already been provided.

An example of this occurred in my office one day when Rob, who had been a patient for a long time, came in frustrated because he had chipped a front tooth. A custom occlusal guard had been made for him, but he was upset and angry and needed to express his anger. Compassion meant that I needed to be with him in sympathy and witness his feelings of frustration without bombarding him with questions like, "Were you wearing your night guard when it happened? Did you bite into something hard?" and quickly recommending treatment: "Well, what's happened has happened, and we can't change the outcome. Let's go ahead and fix the chipped tooth and make you a new night guard." Of course, these are questions that would be

29   Judith, Anodea, *Chakra Balancing: A Guide to Healing and Awakening Your Energy Body,* Louisville: Sounds True, 2004.

relevant for a dentist to ask prior to recommending treatment, but it's not what compassion would say. Compassion would sit and be with the patient and listen at levels II and III. It wouldn't require much time for this patient to feel heard and witnessed. During this time, he would share what he was upset about. He would share what he valued. Once I knew what he valued above anything else, only then would he give me permission to offer a solution to fix this fracture and prevent future fractures from occurring. His acceptance of my treatment recommendation would only occur after I had offered compassion, not before.

Before compassion, I may have reacted to his angry expressions, taken them personally, and even thought to myself, "It's not my job to handle this patient's feelings about chipping his tooth. After all, I didn't break his tooth; he did it by himself by not wearing his night guard or by biting on hard candy." I may have even assumed that he was angry because he had to pay a couple of thousand dollars to fix his tooth and get a new night guard made, whereas money was not why he was upset. This patient was just frustrated because, as he was aging, his dental problems had multiplied in number. Often what we see in front of us in patients is not what's happening underneath, and compassion is a good place to start to unveil what the patient really wants. Let's not forget that compassion for self or others is much easier in the presence of loving-kindness.

On our path to healing, forgiveness is known as the most necessary, and yet, the most difficult work that we must do. If you're human, you have experienced hurt in your past or may be experiencing some in the present. When someone hurts us, we blame them for our pain and don't see the part that we may have played in it ourselves. Naturally, we close our heart, but by doing so, we also close ourselves to giving and receiving love. And by the word "love" here, I don't mean love that exists between lovers. For example, when a team member who you trusted betrays you, that closes your heart chakra. If a patient has been mistreated by a dentist, they may stay frozen in the past, unable to move forward and trust another dentist again. Forgiveness requires the compassion of the heart to understand the forces that may have influenced those who have hurt us. Forgiving ourselves always has to come before we can extend it to others. This doesn't mean that everything we did to ourselves or to others or actions that were done to us by others is blindly condoned and forgiven. But by understanding that every person's essence is separate from the mistakes that they made and that the forces that allowed them to do what they did are unknown to us—by forgiving—we allow ourselves to move forward. We have the choice to refuse to keep carrying the hurtful actions of another and allow our heart to move on. Often, an apology is needed, but even without one, it's our choice not to carry that low energy into our future life.

Sometimes, even a patient may set us up for betrayal. I had a patient once who was very well-mannered and cooperative. I spent a few hours completing six 4+ surface composite restorations on his teeth. There was no indication that he was not trustworthy. He paid for his treatment by check at the completion of the work. I called him that evening to see how he was, and he expressed complete satisfaction with the work. The next day, my bank informed me that he had placed a stop payment on his check. I called him, and he answered the phone. I asked him how he was doing again, and he said he was doing great. I asked him if he was having any problems with the treatment from the day before. He said no, everything was great. I asked him why he had placed a stop payment on his check. He hung up the phone.

Did that make me angry? Absolutely. But I had a choice about how I allowed that incident to affect me. Would I choose to be at cause or effect? I could have remained angry and not trusted any patient who walked into my office from that moment on, or I could see that patient doing me a favor and teaching me a lesson. Although I took him to small claims court only to find out that he had been sued by others for the same reason, he wasn't worth erasing my trust in future patients. I did tighten up my policies as a result, and that never happened again in my practice.

Remaining angry at him would have only hurt me, not him. So, I chose not to carry all the negative feelings that had come from this experience with me. I had to forgive myself for not having systems in place that prevented crimes such as this from happening. Then I had to forgive him because carrying that negative energy would have closed my heart to feeling compassion and love toward the many loyal and wonderful patients who came to my practice and deserved my full compassion and love. Remaining angry would have changed the way I practiced, and I decided that no one would decide that for me. It was by choosing to be at cause and not effect that I refused to be a victim. Love is a feeling, but it is a feeling created out of action. We have to consciously commit at every moment to behave in a loving and caring way toward ourselves and others. Love carries with it generosity, joy, and fulfillment. These were part of my life purpose—what brought meaning to my life. This is yet another reason why it's important to identify what brings you fulfillment and meaning and what the purpose of your work is. Once you define these things, you will see that you cannot be everybody's dentist. When I defined who my ideal patient was, people like the patient who put a stop payment on his check fell off my radar, and I had more time to care for myself and my practice when I didn't have to worry about patients like him anymore.

As part of your radical self-care, take at least a one-week vacation every three months. At first, you might think this is excessive, but before you set the idea aside, try it for six months and look at your numbers compared to the six months when you didn't take a vacation. Please note, your vacations cannot be staying at home and taking care of the yard. They need to be trips away from home where you indulge in caring for yourself, whatever that means to you. Some dentists like to go to a spa and some like to go on a golf trip at a beautiful resort. When you allow yourself radical self-care, your cup becomes so full that you exceed your goals because you have so much to give. You will work harder and more efficiently when you are filling your cup regularly.

If you take anything away from this chapter, I hope it's that you don't have to do this profession that calls for so much from you alone. You have the power to choose to keep your body, mind, feelings, and spirit healthy. These should never be items of negotiation. Change with your body as you age by giving yourself love and compassion. Never allow burnout, depression, addiction, or thoughts of suicide to creep in. You deserve to first take care of you, and it's okay to need help with that. It's okay to be struggling and not know everything, to not have all the answers; it's okay to tell people who can help you that you're struggling. Don't suffer alone in silence: Get help. Asking for help is a sign of courage, not weakness. You matter. You are worth it. You are never a burden. You are a good person. You are enough exactly as you are. The world is a beautiful place because you're in it. You are beautiful. Thank you for existing. Please stay alive and be healthy and well.

Reflection Points

1. Think back to a recent upsetting situation. Ask yourself what you need to forgive yourself for and what you need to forgive in others. Reflect on what love or compassion would say.

2. Choose one exercise that is new for you and add it to your current exercise routine.

3. Schedule one week of vacation in three months and another one three months after that. Track your production and collection during these next six months and compare it to a recent six-month period when you did not take any vacations.

4. Reflect on how you can add buffers of time to your schedule so you can always take a full hour of undisturbed time at lunch to eat and rest.

5. Go to bed early so you can get a full eight hours of sleep every night.

6. Reflect on a time when you were triggered by someone else's behavior or what they said. What was the effect of that on you? These triggers are caused by unresolved emotional wounds. Ask your coach to help you resolve it or seek the help of a therapist who is specialized in this area.

7. Try different meditation techniques until you find the one that resonates with you. Once you find the best one for you, make time for it by adding it to your calendar.

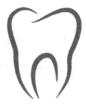

CHAPTER 15:

Obstacles to Profitability

As a dentist and business owner, you face many obstacles on your path to profitability. A significant factor that adds to these obstacles is the flawed viewpoint held by society that magnifies only the perceived rewards of your profession in lieu of recognizing the dedication and hard work required to manifest profitability. If you buy into these misconceptions, you will struggle alone and unnecessarily by allowing obstacles to persist. There are many benefits to looking at the reality of how your practice is performing currently as opposed to how you want it to be. You will discover the most efficient path to profitability as one where you give yourself permission to rise above limitations of thought and thus gain the courage to open up and ask for guidance from a certified professional coach or consultant.

You may find rising above limitations of thought to be your biggest obstacle. Your training has taught you that hard work alone guarantees success. You've seen that to be true over and over again. Therefore, you believe that hard work alone will also guarantee a successful and profitable practice. Let's see if the following recap sounds familiar.

You work extremely hard to get into dental school. You continue to work even harder while going through dental school. Upon graduation, you may or may not decide to continue on in a post-graduation training, such as a general practice residency or a specialty program. Regardless of which post-graduation path you choose, at the end of your training, you are expected to eventually open your own practice and become a rich dentist able to support yourself and your family and plan for retirement. You forego sleep and everything else following the path of every other dentist who came before you, all in the pursuit of establishing a sustainable, profitable practice.

At some point you may find that being profitable is difficult, regardless of how hard you work. This realization is a hard pill to swallow because it's the opposite of the belief that hard work alone guarantees success. If you tell people close to you about your challenges, they will most likely look at you with puzzlement, as though you're somehow flawed. They will tell you to ask your colleagues for advice and what they're doing to be successful, as if you're the only one who doesn't know how to be successful. The feelings of inadequacy will creep in, and in addition to what well-meaning family members say, you will have your own negative monologue in your head belittling and working against you. You will wonder why you can't be profitable when seemingly every other dentist has been. You may even question whether you're missing a productivity gene. You will try to prove to others—and yourself—that you're not weak or less than everybody else by continuing to go to work every day and braving the storm until the signs of stress begin to express themselves in a myriad of ways. As a way to cope with the overwhelming painful stress, you may choose to divert your attention and lessen the pain by drinking alcohol, using other substances, overeating or undereating, or becoming depressed with thoughts of doom and gloom such as: "What if I fail?"

You may confide in your colleagues, but they won't tell you much, not because they don't want to but because they don't know either. They may have their own struggles that they can't talk about and their own belief system and inner dialogue that prevents them from sharing their struggles with you. They might view sharing their negative feelings as a sign of weakness. Your significant other who you've been confiding in may start to get tired of listening to your problems or frustrated because they don't know how to help you. You may decide to turn to your staff members who have prior experience in other offices for help and support. Doing so invites its own brand of problems as it muddies the boundaries between you and your employees (as discussed in Chapter 12). You may do an internet search and find a few coaches and consultants, but just as quickly, you realize you can't afford their high fees.

When you're not profitable, you don't have the extra resources to pay for a consultant or coach. You might borrow money from family or purchase a course providing you with a thick instruction manual of what to do, only to find it six months later in a desk drawer collecting dust. At best, you may put a few of their recommendations into practice with marginal success. There are a few thoughts that repeatedly rotate around in your mind, one of which is that you have invested too much in this career to quit now. Because you're not someone who quits, you keep going to work every day and the problems keep mounting. At some point, you feel stuck. You still love dentistry and being your own boss, but you despise the managing part of this business, so you crumble inside a little every day.

The truth is that the reason you are in this predicament has nothing to do with you and everything to do with how our brains function and the beliefs that were passed down from generation to generation. Let me explain. Our minds are incredibly efficient at helping us survive. Your brain's primary function is to ensure your survival. To reward certain behaviors that ensure survival, dopamine is released in certain pleasure centers of our brain, and the result is a feeling of being high. For example, when we eat, the release of dopamine ensures that we continue to search for food so that we don't die of starvation and our species won't become extinct.

The problem is that in today's society, this reward system is obsolete. Although in the past, dopamine release was linked to our survival instinct, it was never linked to happiness. Desiring the same release of dopamine now whenever we are unhappy can lead to overeating or other negative behaviors that have nothing to do with survival. These behaviors serve to numb the pain that you might be feeling, but they in no way are long-term solutions to ongoing problems that you might be experiencing in your practice—or your life.

In addition, maintaining the same status quo that has kept us alive, regardless of our level of success, is another desire of our minds. Growth in business and profitability is viewed as change, and change is the opposite of status quo; therefore, the mind views change as a threat to its basic survival. So, if you've been running your practice a certain way for a period of time, any change would be viewed as a threat by your mind, so your mind will send signals and messages to ensure that you do things the same way as you always have. The mind cannot discern positive and negative change and is not concerned with whether these activities have brought you profitability. It can only sense that change is not safe. This is often seen in staff members, who have been doing their job a certain way for a long time. Any change to the way they do things threatens their stability. They will especially resist when their boss wants to hire a coach or consultant because they know things will change—and change is threatening to the mind.

I once had a potential client who I was speaking to on the phone. I could tell he had a staff member in close proximity who was also listening to the conversation. After giving him a few sound foundational recommendations to improve the profitability of his practice, I heard this team member interrupt and say, "Why change anything? Just ask her how you can get more new patients."

Suffice it to say, he didn't hire me that day. In twelve months when he called me the second time, he was still looking to increase his practice's profitability by again asking how to get more new patients in the door. This time, I asked to meet him in person without the presence of any of his team members. When we met, after looking at some of his reports, he was able to see that he had close to a million dollars' worth of treatment hidden in the patient files of his existing patients, but because his operation was inefficient, he was not able to access this treatment. Had he spent his hard-earned money bringing in new patients, he would not have been able to maximize the value of those new patients nor would he have been able to discover the potential profit hiding in his existing patients. This is yet another example of how relying on a staff member for business management can be misleading, even when their intention is to help you.

There are many consultants who are not dentists but still have the knowledge to guide you. I have used their services several times and always found their effectiveness to be limited. When they swore up and down that business guidance is based on the same principles whether it's dentistry, physical therapy, or chiropractic, there was always a part of me that didn't trust that statement. As humans, it's important that we are witnessed in our suffering. If someone who proclaims to have the expertise to help you become more profitable, doesn't see the need to listen to what *you* individually are struggling with and the effect of that on your life, they are not the correct advisor for you.

I didn't see how someone who had personally never experienced what I experienced daily was able to tell me how to improve my practice. They didn't know what I went through when treating a patient for five consecutive hours while not only performing excellent dentistry but also being observant and managing their comfort level throughout the procedure. They didn't know what it felt like to not eat or drink or use the bathroom or to keep my body in one position while I drilled on twenty teeth in the same appointment. They would probably say, "Good job, you were profitable that day." But a consultant who has been a profitable practicing dentist themselves, will offer a different type of guidance—one that takes your long-term health goals into consideration even when you can't see the adverse effects of not taking a break for five hours yourself.

The latter would know that profitability in the absence of your health is not worth a penny. The former will only care about your profitability because they would then be paid as a successful consultant that month. In ten years, they most likely will not still be your consultant, and your body's long-term health will not be an issue that they have to consider. They won't even have the vision or the fortitude to know the high likelihood of negative effects if you continue to not take care of your health while trying to be profitable. The lesson here is to make sure when you hire a consultant or coach that they can offer compassion and have experienced for themselves what you are currently going through.

In avoidance of another barrier to profitability, most dental professional liability insurance companies can connect you to a resourceful department that can advise you in order to lower your risk of becoming involved in a legal patient dispute. Because they receive so many calls and they offer a lot of valuable information, you may have to wait to speak to someone. Usually, by the time a doctor calls them, that doctor has been tested to their core by a patient who presents them with a difficult circumstance. The recommendations given in these situations always includes the option to dismiss the patient from the practice. When I was given this recommendation, I often thought that if I dismissed every patient who upset me or my team, I would have been left with only a handful of patients, and profitability would not have been possible with only a handful of patients. From a liability standpoint, that meant that the less patients in my practice, the lower my risk was of getting sued. But the job of these wise advisors did not include asking the dentist how stressed they were before seeing these patients or how many other disastrous events they had dealt with during the course of their day before coming across a difficult patient who had resulted in their call. Their job did not include teaching the dentist how to let go of the negative effects of a difficult situation. As discussed in Chapter 14 and with the help of your coach, by effectively reducing and letting go of stress each day, you can prevent it from accumulating. In addition, by knowing who your ideal patient is and having clear policies in place, when faced with a difficult situation you will be able to see that patient through the eyes of love because you won't lose your center and you won't give it the power to ruin the rest of your day. When you're able to handle difficult interactions from a place of centeredness the negative charge of those interactions will be reduced and you will not need to consider dismissing every difficult patient from your practice. To be clear there are those patients who you need to love enough to let them go so they can find their ideal dentist. However, every difficult patient does not warrant dismissal because some may need more time to trust you—they may even become an ideal patient whose ongoing loyalty will contribute significantly to your profitability.

Contrary to popular belief, when you receive your license to practice dentistry, it does not mean that you have the knowledge to be a successful business owner. If you start your business thinking that you'll learn it just like every other dentist business owner before you, you would be buying into a myth—a false collective belief that could not be farther from the truth. The nature of what we do is difficult, even under the best circumstances. Running a dental practice requires a lot of grit and knowledge that has nothing to do with how smart or excellent a dentist you are. Even if you have grit at the beginning of your career, you will always need to add more. Surprisingly, there are not many resources available to help dentists when they are stressed, which is more often than any of us want to admit.

Even when you are 100 percent convinced that you are ready to ask for help and hire someone like me who can guide you properly and efficiently toward attaining a profitable practice, I want you to know what happens when you make a decision like this. Even when you are well aware that to be more profitable, you will need to modify some—or all—of the ways that you've been running your practice, and even when you are certain that those changes will lead to greater profitability, your mind will not like the change. Your mind will create thoughts such as: "You can do this on your own," or "Why spend so much money for someone to tell you how to do your job, that's embarrassing," or "There are no CE units offered, so are you sure this is worth it?" in an attempt to abort any changes to your routine.

Everyone processes change differently, but having traveled this road already, I can assure you of a few things that are likely to happen. Positive change can only successfully begin when one is seen, heard, and witnessed during both suffering and success over time without judgment. What one person considers suffering or success will not be the same as someone else, which is why my coaching and consulting is never a cookie-cutter process. Think of how many times you've taken CE courses with the intention to incorporate everything that you learned when you return to your office. Even with the best of intentions, all the new information will not be implemented. You will most likely post-pone incorporating the new information within a few weeks of being back. Your back office team will most likely think it's too much work to change routine, and your front office team will know that, as always within a few weeks, it will all be forgotten, and everything will go back to how it was before the course.

In time, you will settle into believing that if you learn and implement just one better technique or one way of improving patient care, efficiency, or profitability, you have done a great job and the course would have been worth it. What you are teaching yourself is that one improvement is better than no improvement.

View the road to profitability as a process, not a one- or two-day event with a thick manual and lots of instructions to take back to your office and stick in a drawer.

You might hear about courses claiming to teach you how to increase your collection to be 100 percent of production in a one-day seminar. Obtaining the information is important, but so is what you do during and after you implement the instructions. Usually, most of what you learn in one- or two-day courses does not result in the long-lasting change that you hoped would occur in your practice, mainly because no one is available to answer the questions that come up for you and your office staff during and after implementation.

Successful implementation of any improvement, especially in the area of profitability, requires ongoing coaching for you as the team leader so that you not only gain the knowledge but learn how to train your team to walk next to you in full support of your practice. During this time, your coach will be your silent partner who will be on your side, offering you continuous guidance for success through the good, the bad, and the ugly. You will no longer feel like your day is consumed by jumping to put out one fire after another. All the other people in your life can return to the role where they are most knowledgeable and appreciated. Your spouse can be your spouse again, and your hygienist can go back to performing her job efficiently without having to listen and try to help you with the array of problems that exist. Regardless of how beaten up you might feel or how impossible you think it might be to be profitable, your coach's job is to consistently hold the reality of your dream of a profitable practice for you, along with holding you accountable to effectively lead your team.

If you are smart enough to make it through dental school, I believe that with the guidance of the right coach and consultant and your full commitment, having a profitable practice can be a reality—not just a dream. If it's not a reality for you yet, I will hold the vision of your dream for you until it becomes your reality too. I will check in and hold you accountable to make sure you always choose and want that reality even more than I do for you. On the way, I insist on having fun and celebrating every single success regardless of size, so that your brain grows to love your soon-to-be reality too.

Reflection Points

1. Describe one current ongoing problem in your practice? How does this problem affect you?
2. What would happen if you solved this problem? How would your practice and your life improve?
3. Have you taken any one- or two-day courses on practice management and profitability? What were you hoping to learn? What are three things that you did learn? Did you successfully implement what you learned? How did your practice improve?

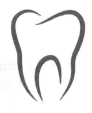

CHAPTER 16:

Conclusion—Beyond the Dentistry

Dentistry is more than just technology, materials, and procedures. At the heart of dentistry is the human connection between the doctor and patient. The human beings who are doing the dentistry with compassion and interaction and connection are the ones healing the patient by listening, the laying of hands, holding space, making the patient feel heard and seen, and so many other things. You are the reason your patients get healthy.

How many times have you successfully delivered excellent dentistry, only to find that if the connection between you and your patient is lost, a year or two later, the dentistry will fail as well? Patient care goes way beyond delivering excellent dentistry. Human connection is the most necessary part of treatment, and that means managing a patient's fears and anxieties, their expectations, their capacity for health, the level of health they feel is possible for them, and their negative beliefs, all of which applies to their families too. Although every year advancements in technology, materials, and delivery methods help us to do our jobs better and more efficiently, we can no longer subscribe to the belief that dentistry alone is the key to helping our patients get healthier.

Most of the people who are attracted to dentistry as a career have type A personalities and are high achievers. They believe in being selfless and will sacrifice themselves in order to serve their patients. With every sacrifice they make, there is a dissolving of the self that can go entirely unnoticed. On the path of being in service to others, their self-worth and identity gets wrapped up in external validation. To get more validation, they work even harder. They may find that eventually they cannot serve their patients because for every hour of treatment, they have to spend another hour on paperwork. This fact alone is the reason they keep hiring more people, but people require management and their hourly rates will increase overhead and eat away at profits.

Frustration and stress mount as they keep hoping that their dream will one day be a reality, so they keep working harder until they are so far removed from themselves that they no longer have a sense of who they are or what they find fulfilling outside of work. The body, however, needs balance. We have been trained to push ourselves when needed, forgetting that even machines need maintenance at regular intervals. There will always be a point when the body will win and we will be forced to look deeper within ourselves to find meaning for what has happened. That is when we ask ourselves: "Why didn't I do something sooner?"

The truth is that to continue caring for your patients and others, you need to care for yourself first. It requires humility to accept your humanity. No one is exempt from illness or burnout or aging. Consider a mouse that is used to going from point A to B to get his cheese every day. If that cheese is moved, the mouse can go from A to B repeatedly all day, working extremely hard, but will end up starving if he doesn't figure out a way to find the new location of the cheese. Maybe the smartest thing he can do is find another mouse who knows the location of many cheese sources and is willing to show him the way. As Spencer Johnson explains so thoroughly in *Who Moved My Cheese*, hard work alone does not guarantee success.[30]

In Chapter 6, I asked you to describe your ideal patient in detail, but doing so does not mean that you should never treat someone who doesn't fit your ideal patient description exactly. I will now ask you to identify what you are exceptionally good at doing. If you're a dentist, you're an expert in dentistry. There are many courses that you can take to hone your skills and increase your efficiency so you can become an even better dentist. This does not mean that you should never take a course in, say, business management. However, with the changing environment that we live in, it is impossible to be great at everything. As a natural perfectionist, this might be hard to take in, but the sooner you realize this, the better your life will be. In this book, I have given you foundational steps you can take to be a profitable dentist, but that does not take the place of working with a coach or consultant for the long-term success of your practice.

I often ask my clients to walk their talk before they ask others to talk and walk the way they do. As leaders, doing something yourself first is key before asking others to do the

---

30 Johnson, Spencer. *Who Moved My Cheese?: An A-Mazing Way to Deal with Change in Work and in Your Life*. New York: G.P. Putnam's Sons, 1998.

same. More specifically, I see people read *Power vs. Force* by David Hawkins (1995) and learn that energy level 200 is the line that separates destructiveness from constructiveness, and they immediately start telling people in their life whether they are above or below the line.[31] They sometimes go as far as saying, "Hey, you need to shift your energy—you're below the line." Rather than taking this approach, it's more effective to notice when you're below the line and try to shift your own energy. By doing this regularly, you will see that people notice a positive change in you and may ask what you're learning. Even if they don't ask right away, they will be wondering about it and when you bring it up, they will be eager to learn because they have seen the positive change in you.

I have been through all the steps of owning, operating, and managing a dental practice. There were days that, in addition to being the doctor, I was the plumber, the cleaning lady, the sterilization assistant … the list is endless. I have had more misfortunes and made more mistakes in my career than I hope any of you will ever experience. And it is hard to be vulnerable. When I share a story about a patient, that patient is a character in my story. What I'm sharing is a story about me where the suffering is real—and so are the lessons. The mask that we wear when we treat patients is very thick, and society supports the thickness of the mask because most patients take comfort in that thickness because it's easier to assume that their dentist is superhuman. What patients don't realize is that their dentist is a human being who has a life outside of their office, a body that has limitations, and feelings that must be addressed. However

---

31   Hawkins, David R. Power vs. Force: The Hidden Determinants of Human Behavior. West Sedona, AZ: Veritas Publishing, 1995.

thick you decide your mask needs to be in front of your patients is your decision, but underneath that mask is someone who needs support so that you don't end up being the mouse who keeps working hard every day for minimal amounts of cheese. The following is an example of a dentist who hired me to find her cheese.

Many dental practices have morning meetings for the purpose of reviewing the day with their team. It had become common practice for every consultant to recommend this to their clients. One of my clients confessed that, although she had been doing morning meetings with her team for years, morning meetings had never worked for her and her team. In the morning, everyone was stressed and rushing to be ready for the day and no one, including my client, was able to be fully present during the meeting. They usually rushed through it, taking quick notes, and couldn't wait for it to be finished so they could go on with their day. My client understood that morning meetings had a worthy purpose, but she felt defeated and upset that they were not working well for her office. After working diligently together to discover who she was and what her needs were, we changed the name of the morning meeting to "Intentional Circle Gathering," where her team came together at the end of the day to review and set their intention for the next day. In addition, each person had to give to and receive from another person on the team one short sentence of appreciation. If anything had upset anyone, they would find a way to release it and let go by shifting their energy to gratitude and joy.

To do this effectively, they had to learn how to experience and express emotions in ways that were healthy and brought life, vibrancy, and great wisdom to each of them individually and as a group. If the upset required additional time for reflection and resolution, they would write a quick note and place it on a branch of a tree, which was basically a folder in the shape of a tree, so that it could be discussed at the appropriate meeting. Once each team member became clear about the intention of this gathering, they started to look for ways that they could appreciate one another during the day. If a problem presented, they would work together to solve it quickly before the end of the day. Everyone became kinder and more gracious to one another. The effect of this gathering was so powerful that it alone was responsible for increasing employee engagement and decreasing turnover in a way that had never been possible before.

This is why I mentioned throughout the book that cookie-cutter programs don't work for everyone. By getting to know this client and her values, we were able to discover together what she needed and how to adjust a meeting that had a useful purpose into one that met her higher purpose and better suited the culture of her practice. This required both coaching and consulting skills.

After reading this book, my wish for you is that you be well on your way to discovering the importance of seeing, knowing, and trusting yourself as a leader. By discovering your values, your boundaries, and what makes your life fulfilling and complete, you will naturally realize with ease, clarity, and confidence the most resonant next steps for creating and maintaining a stress-free and profitable practice. You will know how to hire and retain the right employees, how to identify and attract ideal new patients, how to increase treatment plan acceptance, how to increase production and collection and decrease overhead, how to make sound financial arrangements with patients, and how to decrease no-shows and last-minute cancellations. Your loving, sincere, and calm presence and your ability to foster strong relationships will be appreciated by your patients and reciprocated by their loyalty and many referrals. You will know that you can do all of this on your own, without sacrificing your health and well-being, but you will also know that this will be easier, faster, and more likely to succeed if you hire someone like me as a coach and consultant.

If you're ready to work with me to find the next best version of yourself and become an effective leader, create a five-star team, and consistently manifest profitability in your practice, send me a request through the contact section of my website: www.DrBitaSaleh.com. I can't wait for you to see the results for yourself!

Reflection Points

1. What is your wish for yourself and your practice?
2. What is currently standing in the way of manifesting your wish?
3. Reflect on and decide whether you are ready to engage a coach and consultant so you can manifest your wish easier and faster with more ease and joy.

ACKNOWLEDGMENTS

After more than three decades, there are far too many people to thank individually. But there are those few who cannot go unmentioned.

I want to thank my parents for their unwavering support during all the chapters of my life, both during the good times and especially those times when the path was hard and unclear. Your presence and love meant the world to me.

My depth of gratitude goes to those patients who remained loyal to me through the decades. Thank you for trusting me with your care—you were the reason I showed up every day.

To the Morgan James Publishing team: Special thanks to David Hancock, CEO & Founder, for believing in me and my message. To my Author Relations Manager, Gayle West, for making the process seamless and easy. Many more thanks to everyone else, but especially Jim Howard, Bethany Marshall, and Nickole Watkins for always being available and willing to offer your expertise and support. A very special thank you to Chris Howard—I am grateful for and feel privileged to have had the pleasure of working with you.

While I physically typed away the pages of this book on my keyboard, the spirit of my dog Pumpkin was the one guiding me to write what he so patiently taught me as he enthusiastically accompanied me to work each day—how to care for my patients through the eyes of love. My most loving and heartfelt gratitude goes to him for being my most essential teacher.

ABOUT THE AUTHOR

Bita Saleh DDS, ACC, CPCC, is a general dentist, bestselling author, certified professional Co-Active® coach, business consultant, speaker, and mentor.

Dr. Saleh earned her Doctor of Dental Surgery in 1989 from Herman Ostrow School of Dentistry of USC, followed by a one-year general practice residency at Los Angeles County—USC Medical Center. She has practiced general dentistry in Orange County, California for thirty years and was the CEO of her privately owned dental practice from 1991 to 2017.

Her long-standing interest in complementary and alternative medicine led her to complete a three-year certification in integrative and holistic health (with concentration in energy medicine). Her research, including an innovative four-minute protocol for alleviating dental fear and anxiety by 35% in patients, was published in the *Journal of Energy Psychology* and her bestselling book, *The Well-Referred Dentist*, published by Morgan James presents an evidence-based method to both identify the root cause and alleviate dental fear and anxiety.

Dr. Saleh created The Fearless Way Method to teach and certify dentists to alleviate dental fear and anxiety in their practices. She is now actively and passionately involved in teaching this method to dentists so they can enjoy doing the excellent dentistry they were trained to do without unnecessary stress. This allows them the freedom and space to build trust with their patients, to increase loyalty, and, as an added bonus, increase their practices' profitability.

As an original, enterprising, and forward-thinking certified Co-Active® coach and consultant, Dr. Saleh creates niche programs for her clients based on each client's unique personality, experience, and goals. She is sought-after by many dentists, healthcare providers, entrepreneurs, and coaches for her extensive experience in successful business management and leadership and for her ability to establish patient/client loyalty by creating relationships based in trust.

She currently lives in Southern California where she devotes her time to teaching, writing, coaching, consulting, and looking ahead. To learn more about creating and growing profitable practices and businesses, contact Dr. Saleh at Hello@ drbitasaleh.com.

THANK YOU

Thank you for reading! I admit, the title of this book is a bit misleading. It's about so much more than money and profitability. You may have initially picked this book up and read it to the end because you're interested in increasing your practice's profitability, but by the end you probably realized that you got way more than what you bargained for. While this book does teach you how to be more profitable, it also helps you consider who you are at a much deeper level—a level where your identity is not attached to only being a dentist and/or a business owner.

In designing your authentic practice, I hope you will find your own way of accessing and trusting your intuition, so you can make decisions that are aligned with your mind and heart. By doing so, you will be able to stay at the highest vibration, whatever that looks like for you.

I would love to learn more about you and your experiences in pursuing the career of your dreams. If you want to increase your practice's profitability with ease and joy without losing your health in the process, I want to support you as much as possible in attaining this delicate and most rewarding balance. To show my appreciation to you for reading this book, please visit www.DrBitaSaleh.com to request the following freebies:

1. Grounding meditation link

2. Sample insurance benefits form
3. Sample worksheet for calculating co-payment
4. Sample financial arrangement form
5. Sample inter-office communication form

REFERENCES

Fehmi, Les, and Jim Robbins. *The Open-Focus Brain: Harnessing the Power of Attention to Heal Mind and Body*. Boston, MA: Trumpeter, 2008.

Gerber, Richard. *Vibrational Medicine: The #1 Handbook of Subtle-Energy Therapies*. Rochester, VT: Bear & Co., 2001.

Hawkins, David R., *Power vs. Force: The Hidden Determinants of Human Behavior.* West Sedona, AZ: Veritas Publishing, 1995.

Johnson, Spencer. *Who Moved My Cheese?: An A-Mazing Way to Deal with Change in Work and in Your Life*. New York: G.P. Putnam's Sons, 1998.

Judith, Anodea. *Wheels of Life: A Users Guide to the Chakra System*. St. Paul, MN: Llewellyn Publications, 1987.

Judith, Anodea, *Chakra Balancing: A Guide to Healing and Awakening Your Energy Body,* Louisville: Sounds True, 2004.

Krippner, Stanley, Fariba Bogzaran, and Carvalho André Pércia de. *Extraordinary Dreams and How to Work with Them*. Albany: State University of New York Press, 2002.

Krippner, Stanley, and Debbie Joffie-Ellis. *Perchance to Dream: The Frontiers of Dream Psychology.* New York: Nova Science Publishers, Inc., 2009.

Myss, Carolyn. *Anatomy of the Spirit: The Seven Stages of Power and Healing.* New York: Harmony Books, 1996.

Saleh, Bita. *The Well-Referred Dentist: The Essential Hidden Steps to a Profitable & Anxiety-Free Practice.* New York: Morgan James Publishing, 2020.

Tolle, Eckhart. *The Power of Now: A Guide to Spiritual Enlightenment.* Novato, CA: New World Library, 1999.

Wolman, Benjamin B. *Handbook of Dreams: Research, Theories and Applications.* New York: Van Nostrand Reinhold Co., 1979.